Man is the only creature with the ability to predict, and then act to take advantage of those predictions. Futurlogics is the system of thought that will perfect these innate processes. Futurlogics is prospective thinking, designed to free the mind to think as it should. Because the future is the potential of man, the intelligent use of that future is the maximum the mind can achieve!

Glossary

Futuring: noun: The mental consideration of the future as a concept, as a potential reality, and as all that is yet to be in actuality.

Futur: verb: The activity of futuring.

Futurus: Latin: for about to be, about to exist.

Logic: Latin/Greek: for logic, rationale, reasoning, inference, sanity, system of reasoning: Aristotle's logic, mode of reasoning.

Now defining by combining futur + logic + S creates the new word:

FUTURLOGICS

The is an "S" in FuturlogicS because there is plurality in the future, to a person or to the society, because of the choice or choices they make. A singular future with no detours is known only by God the Father and those Saints and Prophets He reveals this information. Since we are not HE or THEY, the future is dependent upon free will and agency. Futurlogics will always be plural with an S.

FUTURLOGICS: MOS: (M)ind (O)perating (S)ystem

What is a **MOS**? In computer science an **OS** is an acronym for **(O)perating (S)ystem**. An Operating System provides a base to put various apps or applications to execute. The Mind/Brain also needs an Operating System upon which we can function with what we know. It is how we apply our knowledge, either upon knowledge itself or upon the things we know about. It is theory in action. A **MOS** or *(M)ind (O)perating (S)ystem* is the theme upon which we execute our methods or praxis.

FUTURLOGICS

A System of Prospective Thinking:

by james n. hall

Printed
in the
United States of America

SELF TEACHING PUBLICATIONS
WEST JORDAN, UTAH 84084
USA
www.futurlogics.com

Futurlogics – 4 – *A System of Prospective Thinking*

to Juliet Esther

Acknowledgments

I am indebted to many persons and feel to name a few whose help contributed greatly to the completion of this work.

A grateful thanks to Joyce Davis for the preliminary preparation of the manuscript.

I also consider the final proofing of Pat K. Hilder invaluable.

Thanks also goes to Cary Smith and Cris Larsen for the conversations on the Futurlogics theory and applications.

Cliff Kemple's graphics skills brought cover design to life; again thanks.

Lastly my children's unfailing faith in me gave me the necessary hope and pride in the future. 1983

Additional Thanks to the following:

My Grandpa who was a candy maker and could lift 600 lbs.

My Grandpa who was part Cherokee and took me hunting and fishing.

My Grandma who love to cook and love her grandchildren.

My Grandma who spoke Hebrew and five other languages and loved her grandchildren.

My Children who have have watch me write and teach Futurlogics all their lives. They are evidence of my success.

My Grandchildren - - my proudest work.

My wife Julie O. Hall has helped to write, discuss, theorize, critique, contribute, suggest as my sounding board, more thanks than can be expressed.

Thanks. 2013

SELF TEACHING PUBLICATIONS
UTAH, USA

**** Table of Contents ****

PART THREE
Application

PREFACE

This book is not just about the future. It also concerns what man *thinks* and *believes* his future to be. We *plan, prepare, wait,* and *predict.* Why? The rationale behind these activities is taken for granted. The future is such a necessary part of the thinking process, it behooves us to make an in-depth study of it. By so doing, one may reveal to himself that the future is a prime ingredient to life.

Yet, an exact knowledge of the future seems beyond us, like tomorrow's sunrise. But all have preconceptions of the future, even if they are guesswork. Yet living requires pragmatism. In turn, a practical idea of the future is needed to match problems that arise. Don't we demand to know the time and place for every potential event and condition? Specific time and place however, frustrates an overall study. This untempered demand of specificity is too much too soon. Much could be gained through studying the general properties and characteristics of the future; afterward, we may be in a better position to make the more difficult predictions. We will learn that the prerequisite to prospective thinking is the ability to think in the *most general of terms.*

We presently have a rudimentary prescience from trial and error. In no way will Futurlogics detract from these empirical beginnings. In fact using what we already know, to expand consciousness and awareness, is fundamental to this thesis. Nevertheless, by necessity there must be some unlearning of methods that detract from a more expansive approach. Unfortunately, unlearning is harder to do than learning from a fresh start. Therefore the heart of the generalist or futurist must have courage and mettle.

This means that the thinking system of futurlogics is the capping off of education and the beginning of the self teaching principle. It takes us back to the preschool state of mind, when the most prolific learning rate existed. Learning then was natural and easy, but somehow this ease has become dormant and almost forgotten. The aims of this book include the reactivation of the art of learning to the ideal.

Futurlogics is presented as a self-improvement book, as the subject of the future lends itself to the technique used in that class of writing currently published. The reader may find it helpful to view this work in the same format as a self-improvement book, to realize the goals presented. Most self-improvement books are "now" oriented however, formulated to improve status, prestige, and power. Instead, Futurlogics will go ahead to the future, really seeking the success promised in these other books. Accomplishing our goals should be easier and viable.

It must be understood that this book contains no prophesy, no predictions or forecasts of any kind, except those used merely to exemplify the inherent principles of prospective thinking. In no way are they to be interpreted as mystical and underlying the pattern of things to come—except in the most general way. If one is seeking such, he will have to look elsewhere, as one of the tenets of this book is that the future must be a matter of self-discovery, and not the prerogative of a select few dictating their vision to the many. Self-teaching must remain the core and wellspring of this writing. And the interpretation of religious writings should be left to those who have the authority to do so.

james n. hall 1983

Some editing has been done in this edition by the author himself and his wife Julie. Perhaps more is needed, but for those who wish to explore the unknown and the future, sufficient is more or less is more. The original discourse and intent was preserved. The additions and corrections were meant to clarify and enhance the original printing. The hazards and beauties of self-publishing were maintained. One of the hazards is that the creator of ideas must also edit, proofread, design the layout etc.. This is also the grand beauty of self-presented work as it remains original. I love self-publish works now, as every mistake is a beauty mark on a virtuous girl.

james n. hall 2013

PROLOGUE

MATERIALITY

We are surrounded by the dimension of **matter**. Everything seems to be made of it. We need only look at our own body to see the importance of materiality in our lives. It is so overpowering, that it is the common denominator of existence. With some individuals materiality is so dominant, that every facet of life begins and ends in its dimension. All of us find our senses focused to the aspect of the properties of the material dimension. Matter provides data which looms in our consciousness.

The opposite of matter is **space**, and space is equally important. Where the photographic negative is black, the positive is white. Likewise, the negative copy of matter is space. Where there is no matter, there is space. Space is opposed in every respect by materiality.

Again, where there is no space there is matter. Our sensory organs cannot perceive space directly. Rather they only perceive where matter ends. We judge space as mirrored from matter, as we do with the photographic negative and its opposite, the positive print.

If the environment were only made of space and matter its aspect and panorama would be fixed and still, but such is not the case. Reality is not and inanimate snapshot. Motion, change, life are evident, all pointing to the very important third element—**time**. This central dimension of existence turns, the still snapshot photographically into the flowing movie. Our environment consists of **matter, space and time**. And time is the "magic" of motion. And the motion of matter in space defines energy.

Within the dimension of time, there is an indenture we call NOW. The environment in that instant constitutes present reality. We perceive it with our eyes, ears, nose, through all of the senses. Our body anchored by its materiality must continue in this moment of NOW—but intuitively we know that things exist beyond immediate materiality. There is an awareness that time extends reality to its upper reaches. If the mind were not fettered by matter, it could soar through time! At the beginning, materiality fetters our mind's imagination.

Don't we feel all things are going somewhere? We have become aware of the new relationships surrounding us. The material aspect changes when things are viewed through the perspective of temporality. With time there is progress and expansion, indeed the addition of time to the thought process liberates the mind to think as it should, freeing it from the confines of materiality.

Life is the ultimate reality. Life consists as a span of time, a planet, and a mind full of thoughts. These three spheres constitute the total environment—namely the temporal environment. The physical and the mental conjointly complete all the dimensions of life. However time is the abstract relationship of the other dimensions, and it eludes simple sensory observation. Because of this, the temporal environment and time must be studied with a special technique. Futurlogics will teach us that technique.

THE FUTURE IS THE SUBJECT
AND
OBJECT OF OUR RESEARCH

The most fascinating part of our temporal environment is *our* future. This future is the subject of our thoughts and the object in our living. However, when *the* future is mentioned, we feel either a pleasant stirring or an uneasiness, exciting the mind to its potential. The degree of intelligence we use, alone limits any probe of *the* future. A system is needed to utilize our intelligence in an organized study of *our* future or *the* future. An **MOS** if you please. Futurlogics is such an approach. The future exists only in the mind of man until it is observable. If we cannot predict the future, then we must apply Futurlogics to study what we believe the future to be.

Positive "mental attitudes," "thinking big," "self-improvement programs," suggest that we are guided by our beliefs. Without understanding the future, we are in danger of losing the potential and the latent talents we possess. After all the goals we choose, come from our belief in what the future might be. Understanding the future and mastering Futurlogics assists us in achieving our goals. To do this we must think big, be positive, and accept progress.

THE NEED TO KNOW

The future is not what it used to be. The past is no longer prologue. This is an unprecedented age and it will be difficult to find examples in history to parallel what is happening now—let alone what will happen in the near future!

In times past our influence upon our environment, has had the impact of a butterfly upon a rock. Now, we are like the bull in a china shop. Brute force offers immediate solution; but the side effects of using force blindly, mount to threatening levels. Modern technology has delivered into our hands such power, that we literally can change the shape of the planet we reside upon. We fight nature rather than, use her forces to work for/with us. We expend too much energy, when nature would supply our needs.

We needn't be so brutish. Instead, we can profit from a studied look at the ways we deal with the future. If we envision turmoil and confusion ahead, the affects/effects of our assumptions influence all of our activities, and what we believe the future to be, may directly cause those things to occur. Moreover, imagination flourishes when so little of the nature of the future is known. History books verily proliferate upon library shelves, but books concerning the future stand out as oddities. Alternatively, accepting ignorance is to accept the consequences of that ignorance!

POTENTIAL OF THE SYSTEM

Although this approach to the study of the future is new, there is a familiar ring to each idea. These ideas are in reality, very old ideas seen in a different light. Updating old ideas can be repackaged now as new ideas. There was a time when prophets were respected and their gift acknowledged. Futurlogics promises to restore this respect as it brings the future into the range of common sense. Experience is the basis of this approach, thus we are able to keep the study within the reach of everyone, and not only touch an esoteric group of Futurists. Because the future affects all of us, we need to be "tuned in." We need our mind to be informed in a new paradigm.

Latent within each of us are many talents and capabilities which are gifts at birth. Many of these innate capacities will never be discovered if they are not developed. Futurlogics expands the mind, revealing latent potential. The mind is the first and the last frontier. It is the ultimate horizon.

*MAN IS THE UNIT OF MEASURE

When man begins to measure an object he uses a rule with a scale to compare the dimension of measurement. What does man use to measure the universe and the things he sees in it? The standard unit by which man will measure anything is ultimately himself. Man will eventually relate all things to himself. Man himself is the standard, from which he will gauge everything he encounters or will encounter. Recognizing this therefore must be the key, to understand the things man attempts to know and discover.

The rule is most evident when man studies himself or his fellows. He will compare himself to all others and arrive at a norm or a *standard of reference,* to be able to predict or judge the behavior of the individual or society. This standard of reference can be distilled to be the bank of accepted knowledge acquired and recorded. Finally knowledge is used to measure knowledge.

This principle can be further refined, until we arrive at the level of an axiom or a postulate, which is that man uses current knowledge to measure and research the unknown. Put more simply, the known is used to gauge and measure the unknown. Present accepted knowledge is the unit of measure, by which all other knowledge known and unknown is weighed and judged.

Even taking one step further back we find that the mind is both topographer and cartographer, of all that thought surveys. Therefore, understanding the mind is key to mapping out knowledge. The study of the mind remains an essential to any subject. Since the subject is the future, we will have to investigate the mind itself.

It is said the mind of man contains the past, present, and future all at once. If this is so, then the mind of man contains the complete map of reality. We must refer and reflect upon the workings of the mind. Psychology investigates the mind. However, its range is limited to study the "visible aspects" of thinking. Futurlogics imposes no such limit.

*Man is both male and female as neither can surpass the other in intelligence. By no means is the future exclusive.

PART ONE

Orientation:

Chapter I

PSYCHOLOGY

ATTITUDE OF FUTURLOGICS

Research in the field of psychology has produced little organized knowledge, of the ways in which we comprehend the future. Much of the thinking we do about the future is indirect, akin to the subconscious thought processes common to psychology in general. The reason for this is, that sustained conscious thought of the future produces anxiety. This anxiety however, is caused more from lack of a concrete design, than by reason of the abstract nature of the future. A solid method will allay uncertainty; we will learn uncertainty can be very productive to creative thought.

It is commonly said that "the best way to handle the future is by not thinking of it at all." Some social and cultural influences foster such approaches by indirect means. Even so, not thinking of the future is another way of saying that we are relinquishing conscious effort, letting our forethinking remain at the subconscious level.

When a subconscious and suppressed idea is brought to consciousness, it will either produce anxiety and distress, or it will relieve tension and be cathartic. Therefore, a certain amount of tension is unavoidable, but there will also be rewards to exhilarate and stimulate study. Future studies can be fun.

Our method of defining our surroundings has a lot to do with our attitude. Attitude can also turn anxiety to serenity and make the discordant become harmonious. Compare the man who sees a glass of water as half empty, to the man who "knows" it to be half full! A positive or negative view illustrates the effect of definition in thinking and in perception.

The future should never be defined as "half empty," as a positive attitude is to be favored at first while searching the future, thus contributing to the full benefit of futurlogics. Pessimism versus optimism is an old debate, and we have heard the benefits and detriments of either emphasized. Later, we will see that these are merely tools of the good futurist. They must not be accepted as the complete approach. In the meantime, we are to remember while assuming the positive or the optimistic stance, how we define our world will influence how we live in the world. Let us be positive with our definitions.

Everything flowing in time has either a beginning, middle or ending, depending upon our definition or point of reference. In reality, what is a beginning of one is the middle of another, also what is the middle of some other is the ending of still another. Until we realize the power that definitions have over our attitude, we will not understand that beginnings, middles and endings are at the same time endings, middles and beginnings. All of this has much to do with our ability to study the future. Some persons see every event as an ending; this will foster a doomsday attitude leading to a negative outlook, which is not always useful. Again, those who see the middle of every action are sensory bound, and value is measured in terms of material hard reality. The beginning-man is the one in the best position because, he has the perspective of seeing everything progressing in its natural time order. He may conceive the whole of reality as it develops in sequence—first to last. Yet, when is *the* beginning? Again, it is a matter of definition, if not perspective and attitude.

THE MIND AND THE BRAIN

The synergy of mind is more than the brain. Thinking is a stimulus in itself. The mind responds to more than sense perceptions of the physical environment. Thinking can cause more thinking. Even animals react to the internal stimuli of their instincts. Man uses his intelligence to survive and progress, as animals use their instinct to adapt and survive changes in their environment.

We will not assign limits to mental capacity, since doing so causes artificial barriers. We will discover the natural limits of the mind by personal experience, and avoid any skeptical closed-mindedness that retards mental growth. Be optimistic! The mind may have no limits!

RELATIONSHIP OF THE MIND TO THE SENSES

Many animals have a keener sense of sight, smell, or hearing than man does. It would logically follow that animals are in better contact with the environment. But sense perception without mental process is nothing more than stimulus-response of rudimentary form.

Animals perceive no past and no future. They only have instincts to enable them to operate in the continuum of the present. Man not only has the ability to conceive of a past and a future, but he can also consciously plan and prepare for future events and conditions. His intelligence makes possible a life beyond simple sense contact with the physical environment.

On the other hand, without senses the mind operates in a vacuum. When our sensory contact is limited, we compensate for it by relying on the other senses, as we observe in the blind and deaf. During sense deprivation experiments, the effect of sensory deficiency upon consciousness is dramatic. When the mind is cut off from sensory feedback, it goes into action with new freedom, but as time passes progressive boredom and hallucinations result. Although it is refreshing to imagine an environment free of distraction, the mind thrives and needs stimulation. We meditate at times, and "sightsee" at other times, and less imaginatively we "site-see." The art of balancing the mental life with the sensory life is the key to concentration and observation. If our mind is engrossed in deliberation like the absent-minded professor, we miss many things that go on about us. But it is obvious that if we don't stop to consider, ponder, meditate, we may never know the meaning of things.

Beyond the range of sight, hearing, smell, taste and touch, we are at a loss—apparently. We have invented instruments to compensate for these limitations. We see the stars through telescopes and listen to fish sending signals through the water with a sonar device; through instruments our ancestors never knew existed. But, when instrumentation reaches its limits, we are forced to rely again on the mind and the purely mental contact.

The future is total abstraction. It is something that must be grasped by the mind itself, and the mind must be at its best to consider the future. Prospective thinking is the most advanced form of thought. The future must be approached from a purely mental environment; ultimately, we must perceive the future with our mind.

The senses only give us a sample of the things they perceive, and they never tell us everything. Even if we are outfitted with perceptual organs to provide us information of the material world, their inherent limitations give us only a partial picture of what is "really out there." (Note: what is physically out there, may be different from what is actually out there.) The magician uses this fact to work his feats of illusion. Also, no two persons receive the same event exactly the same. We are never able to see, hear, taste, smell, or touch everything all at once. Yet, we interpret what we see, hear, taste, smell or touch by what is in the mind. Since everyone knows different things, they see, hear, taste, smell and touch differently.

The senses alone leave us with an incomplete picture of the total environment.

Reality is "seen" with both, the mind and the senses. We can make up for this partial contact with the material environment, by the mental process. From samples we derive the properties of the whole. The mind uses the samples as data to "fill in," and we feel we have the complete picture.

Since observation is never complete, things are understood only after we have accumulated data from many perceptive angles, from many periods of time and many sources. This is converted into a symbolic form so the mind can operate upon it. From symbolic form we gain the capacity to judge, to value, to remember and relate to any subsequent perception by adding depth. Perception becomes more meaningful, as the number of related experiences give supportive background to sensory data.

The first impressions and experiences—though superficial—are always a sample—let this condition be a new word: *samplary.* We remember the first time we experience things better than the succeeding times. When we let the dominating influences of a strong first impression color the following similar experiences, we often make poor judgments. Sometimes this is used to our benefit, such as when favorable first impressions foster important relationships. When we meet a new business contact we are on our best behavior, and the red carpet is rolled out to dignitaries to cement this effect.

THE MIND AS PERCEIVER

The mind is the receiver of perception, since it accepts and registers the stimuli sent by all the other senses. We can use common expressions to illustrate this: i.g. that "beauty is in the eye of the beholder," "music is in the heart," and "seeing is believing." The mind adds quality to perceptions of the sense organs. With out these additions to sensory contacts, we would be at the basic stimulus reaction of the lowest forms of life. Action would be merely reflexive.

Many of us need a place to meditate. Remember the last time the radio or the television was on in the next room, while you were trying to read or concentrate? In such a din we say, "I can't even hear my own thoughts." Thinkers, writers, and students seek a place where they are able to tune into their own thoughts.

It is common practice to avoid stimulus and perception, mostly for beneficial reasons, contributing to study habits. But what else do we block out, or shield from consciousness? Do we put out of mind other things as easily, such as the perceptions of the mind itself? Can the mind receive on its own, directly from the environment? Does a direct mental perception occur, bypassing the regular channels? Perhaps we ignore more than we realize. Can we be conscious of more than our own thoughts? Does the mind learn by direct means? Answers to these questions fairly scintillate the mind.

DUAL DEFINITION OF DMP

At this point in our discussion a conceptual idea fundamental to Futurlogics must be introduced. Direct Mental Process and Direct Mind Perception, (DMP), both refer to a mental operation necessary to self-teaching and learning the future. The mind as a "perceptual organ" itself, is an idea that opens to view the world beyond the five senses. The future is intuitively known and the concept of Direct Mental Process and/or Direct Mind Perception takes on special meaning, offering answers (perhaps to easily and temptingly) we seek. However, DMP is basic to this study. (Or to researching the unknown in general. The future can be a one word metaphor for all that is to be researched or yet learned.) And DMP is a very useful tool.

DMP is a duplex acronym of both (**D**)irect (**M**)ind (**P**)erception and (**D**)irect (**M**)ental (**P**)rocess. The definition of **DMP** must be left purposely ambiguous to draw in simultaneously both dimensional features of mental consciousness. The rational and intuitive nature of thought are both necessary to prospective thinking. Because **DMP** contact with the future is left loosely defined, personal input into the subject is unavoidable. Rather than being a problem, such bias is an aid (if we keep an open mind). As we shall see, as the theory develops, **DMP** can only be a matter of self-discovery and intuition, after we develop insights into Futurlogics.

DMP may be creativity, meditation, intuitive insight or a process yet undefined. At this point we cannot make a strict definition. The definition of **DMP** is a matter of continual self discovery. If we say what it IS, we also say what it IS NOT, and the mind is not left free to make its own discoveries and experiences, necessary to Futurlogics and to self-teaching. It is offered as a temporary concession that, since we now know that a future exists, we must have come to this knowledge by a purely mental process or perception. What that is, is **DMP**! If you know there is a future, then it came through **DMP**.

Before **DMP** is apparent by self-discovery, we experience hunches, insights, precognition and similar phenomena which reflect(s) one form of bias; conversely, training and schooling in logic and reasoning and philosophy-related experience, might ascribe to **DMP** the reasoning processes necessary to handle abstract thought. Either view or input is constructive to an understanding of Futurlogics and **DMP**. If an open mind is maintained, these inputs will be unavoidable with an open definition, but this should not affect the study of Futurlogics. Diversity of this nature should enhance the learning effect, when principles of Futurlogics are discussed with others, who look both at the concept of the future and the future itself with interest.

No matter what **DMP** means to the reader, the general concept is a tool in studying the future. The minimum limits however for a working definition, is that the future or the temporal environment can only be mentally considered or perceived. **DMP** offers a quick reference to such demands upon higher thought processes (metacognition.) **DMP** is also the intuitive process of hunches and insights that bode of the future. Finally, it is a shortened description of all the means of learning exclusive of the five senses.

Seeing is believing, but what we believe directs our eyes toward what we see. Without **DMP** we would not learn even with the five senses.

As we study the six modes/models of Futurlogics, we shall see how nicely the three modes that relate to the time continuum equate to **D**IRECT **M**ENTAL **P**ROCESS namely past, present, future; and how appropriate the other three modes relate to **D**IRECT **M**IND **P**ERCEPTION because of the principles of intelligence they represent namely imagination, assumption/waiting, creativity. This form of parallel thought streaming in **DMP** become(s) foundation(s) to the holistic mind. **DMP** *is plural and singular at once.*

DMP DEPENDS UPON CONSCIOUSNESS

Can we ever be conscious of everything at once? Awareness is limited, attention can be distracted, diverted and blocked. There is always an area of oblivion in mental life. There are limits. We have levels of consciousness, fields of awareness, directions of attention. These are dimensions of mind as they are dimensions of **DMP**. What one person may be acutely aware of, another may be totally oblivious towards. Intelligence, native abilities, and capacities vary from person to person. Individually, we vary in intelligence at different times. We may go through all the phases of consciousness in a day. During the night in sleep, early in the morning, late in the evening will find most persons in different moods, if not different mental states of consciousness or awareness. Experiments have shown that there are persons who perform at test better in the morning, while others will do better in the evening, and what we are alert to at one time of day, we may miss altogether at another time. Consciousness is a changeable thing.

Nevertheless, we may be more aware than we think. Blocking out unwanted stimulus is habit. We shut out distractions to concentrate. Does concentration get out of hand, so that we also repress other mental activities, we feel to be nonsensical or irrelevant? The extent of repression and blocking is unknown. Remember scientists have determined that we use only a small percentage of our total brain capacities.

Latent within us may be things we need only dream about to make true.   Allow your intuitions!   Ideas that pop into consciousness may be developing insights that will free flow to the surface. Attention to all things which enter the mind is the key to **DMP**. We must trace the origin of all ideas to their source. When we can do this, we know the credentials of our beliefs and knowledge.   Besides, giving true credit to the origin of ideas, improves the imagination and creativity.

(Author's Note: Things in the future(s) and in **DMP** are plural and singular at the same-time or at-once, making English rules very difficult   to follow.   Language rules of a society will shape the perception of the future(s) that could be "seen."   It is important to realize the impact that language and education have upon what is "viewed" in futurity. 2013)

Chapter II

LEARNING

THE ABILITY TO DO THE BEST WITH THE LEAST

Every time we learn something new, we suspect that there is more to know ahead in time or out there. Also, when we discover falsehood once believed as true, there is a regret we have been deceived. We question, "what else do we believe that is false?" Sometimes we just make mistakes. In short we are constantly learning and deducing there is even more to learn.

The activity of consciousness is increased, when we become aware of all we do not know. Facing the unknown will cause the mental conscious to be more self-directed, as we try to fill in what we do not know. Solving a problem with plenty of information requires less thought than, when we try to solve problems with sparse data. None of us can ever know it all; therefore, it is safe to conclude that we may always be making decisions and solving problems with inadequate information. Indeed realizing this, is the beginning of mature thought.

There is a saying that "to be educated you should know many things, but to be wise you must be aware of what you do not know." Surveying the extent of our ignorance is a prudent approach to learning. Like the ostrich who thinks he is hiding when he puts his head in a hole, the comfort in believing that you know all the answers is false security. Accepting ignorance is the first step a person must take to be teachable, let alone to be able to learn by self study.

We approach problems and decisions somewhere between a vacuum and a solid foundation of adequate information. How we handle things in an atmosphere of partial knowledge is fundamental to progress and learning—especially learning the future. The future is what is not yet known. In an age of information overload, less can be more.

Each individual varies in ability to make good decisions or judgments in the face of imperfect data. Ask a leader how he makes good decisions and he will tell you he must think ahead by anticipation. We expect leaders to make decisions when no one else can. In fact, good leaders have the uncanny knack of making decisions, when no one else has enough information to go on. If everything was obvious to all, no leadership is required.

The qualifications for good leadership are self-confidence, forethought, energy, and the ability to do well when others are at a loss. Good leadership is more than the result of self-confidence. Though it is true that the self-confidence of the leader will give the bewildered follower a sense of security, the unstated characteristic of his success is the special gift that supports that confidence. The leader must face the unknown with a method or it will be sensed by his followers. The strength of leadership lies in the ability (or gift) of making good decisions from insufficient data. The trust put in this skill leads to self-confidence, which in turn comforts the follower and supports his confidence that the leader can face the unknown.

Not only do leaders make decisions and plans for the future, but everybody must sometime look ahead. It is in our best interest to learn the skill(s) to do better with less. We must avoid falling into the trap of thinking all our judgments and prejudices are based on a complete knowledge. Because in this book, we are interested in the future, and how to deal with it, we should acquire *the ability to do the best with the least*. Indeed, it is a principle essential to Futurlogics. This will measure our intelligence.

In goes without saying, that truth is a thing we must seek. But we seem to always know less than we should. We still are ignorant and unknowing of much. It seems to be a permanent condition. However, the optimum use of ignorance or innocence is true learning. But to have faith in anything that is not true is destructive and discredits faith and its promotion of intellectual growth. If faith is to be of any good use, it should lead us to the knowledge of the truth. *Ability to do the best with the least* can be one definition of faith. Faith is an ability to deal with insufficient facts and data, doing it so we live as successfully as if we were fully informed. Faith makes life actionable.

That "a little knowledge is a dangerous thing" is a true statement. But we are forced to work with what we have. (Or another way of saying this is that specialists often do not consider the larger picture, and may disregard the focused view impact upon the greater field of concern or its environment.) The time required to gain perfect knowledge would be more than the normal life span. Ignorance is a condition that will be with us for a long time. To offset this condition, we will have to learn skills of making decisions and acting in a climate of partial knowledge. Doing the best we can is not enough. We will have to do better than we can, or we won't progress. Forethought, planning and preparation are the essence of doing the best with the knowledge we have now, and all of these activities are based upon prediction.

We are not just talking about being a good guesser. Some persons seem to have developed an innate skill. They live and act as if, they are better informed. They are not just echoing the consensus; but they are thinking and responding from something within themselves. This suggests that **DMP** is working for them, because of the absence of external means used to make wise decisions. When a decision is in the balance, the "something" that tips the scales is, an intuitive insight that is akin to inspiration. Such things defy explanation; one must experience such an insight to understand it.

"A little knowledge" can also make faith grow abundantly. Faith should be the foundational soil from which knowledge grows. A faith that does not make a person more knowledgeable and less dependent is sterile. Faith is the preliminary operation of the mind that results in knowledge.

Faith in science, education, and human rights can be an attitude that will realize a better civilization and greater knowledge. Faith in oneself produces the positive mental attitude described in books concerning self improvement. It must be emphasized here, that stubborn adherence to ignorance is not faith. Faith is readiness to absorb what is not easily seen. It is the mental "gift" of learning, of turning to the heighten state of consciousness, that is produced when we finally realize our knowledge is imperfect and our data insufficient, to make the decisions crucial to progress and survival. When we are forced to move ahead, our thoughts must reach out for the answers. This reaching out is the basis of faith and **DMP** which complement each other.

LEARNING

Applying the principle of "*doing the best with the least,*" or faith. We should grow in knowledge and experience. Learning is the means to gain knowledge. The standard of living that we have attained is based upon our knowledge of, and ability to deal with, our environment. Thus, *how* we learn becomes the most important thing to learn. At some stage of growth, we must be our own teacher to continue. Eventually, we must research to go further.

Schools and institutions of learning are common and necessary, and we are required by law to attend school from childhood. Status in the community is based, to a large extent, upon our schooling. We must even be trained to live in our modern society.

There is a variance in the amount of knowledge that each individual obtains. Acquiring knowledge is due mostly to learning approaches rather than native ability to learn. As two persons of equivalent ability, but with differing approaches to learning, will achieve different amounts of knowledge, so learning how to learn can increase the efficiency of learning rate. If we can learn only when taught by a teacher, we are blocked from the ultimate source of knowledge— ourselves. It is true that we can hire teachers to help us, but the problems come when we try to learn the things, that the teacher has yet to learn! New discoveries must be made by accident, or by those who have learned of/by themselves. This ability which we know as **DMP**, is the technique of gaining knowledge without a teacher. Teachers are essential to pass on the knowledge of the past, but they cannot teach us of things yet to occur, or that have yet to be discovered and printed in a textbook.

Existing educational systems are so powerful that we have drowned in their successes. We are led to believe it is a fact that we can learn, only through the "system" and its teachers alone. And this belief stifles the innate ability, the gift we possess from birth, to learn how to learn by ourselves. Sometimes this ability to learn to learn, is called metacognition. The more you know the more you can know.

Sooner or later, need will force us to learn through the intuitive process of **DMP**. This is the time when our education reaches its limits. School has ended and life begins. Education becomes a base of operations if it contributes to discovery, or a block, if it impedes or interferes with discovery. Education should extend our vision, and not blind us with narrow-minded perspectives burdened with prejudice. What we already know should aid us in learning additionally.

UNIVERSAL PRINCIPLE(S)

In most university curriculum, prerequisite courses are necessary before entering advanced classes. The more complex the class, the more preliminary background classes must have been taken. The principle that greater knowledge is based upon lesser knowledge is nearly universal, and is not restricted to the school systems. Every businessman learns that it takes money to make money. The more money we have to start a business, the easier it is to make it a profitable venture—all things being equal. In health, the best way to remain healthy is to start healthy when young. Generally, he who has shall receive. And he that receives can receive even more. This is the universal principle.

(We might add here that the quality of what we accept as knowledge greatly influences what we receive—we are familiar with the effects of being falsely informed. Accepting a false-hood as truth has been an ageold cause of great human suffering. Conversely accepting a truth as a lie, can cause just as much damage. It is one thing to be deficient in knowledge, money, health, etc., but it is another thing to think we have something, when we do not and be deceived. Enterprises based upon unsound principles, falsehoods, superstitions, myths, or dogmas will be a poor base(s) from which to continue further research. Such things can only lead to confusion and loss. To know more of the future, we must have correct knowledge from which to begin.)

Knowledge and **DMP** will become inseparably connected. We need the knowledge to focus attention, awareness and the state of consciousness to the future. But mental contact with the future is useless unless we have the understanding to grasp our extended "vision." New knowledge may be misunderstood without the right prior knowledge to base it upon. Everything either works together or pulls apart, when we turn our minds towards the future. Our *ideas of the future* are either based upon synergy or its opposite deception. When these *ideas* are founded upon deception there is discord at a minimum.

The *"more we have the more we can have"* is the universal principle that operates in all phases of life and thought. This principle is the key to **DMP** or any other form of learning by individual study. When we understand the nature of the universal principle, we can then begin to see the process of **DMP,** then intuitive learning is understood and can be used effectively.

For centuries every new custom or invention has met opposition. During the dark ages persecution and death were the rewards of private research that brought forth new knowledge. Galileo was not warmly received as he formulated and made public his findings. The "learned community" of his time threatened his life and forced him to make a public retraction of his discoveries. Leonardo Da Vinci had to write in cryptic notes to prevent censure, from those who were organized to maintain the status quo.

Today, we have seen the results of invention and innovation in scientific research. New ideas are welcomed, more than they have been at any time in history. The attitude that new discoveries are useful and not a threat, has changed us for the better. We know now, that all ways of learning are of value—if they produce results.

Self-educated persons are rare, but they have contributed greatly to our store of knowledge. The greatest thing we could learn from the self-educated is often ignored as their success is celebrated. What we miss is the manner in which they have taught themselves. When we marvel at their accomplishments, we conclude that it is a sign of their genius. Essential to learning the future is the principle of the self-taught genius.

All new knowledge initially learned from the surface will not match what we already know. Genius is the ability to simplify the new knowledge within the body of existing knowledge, so that all can understand it. Often we block many new ideas from our consciousness because we feel them to be ridiculous, impertinent, irrelevant, illogical, worthless, out of the ordinary, out of order, intrusive, etc., because we don't penetrate the surface to the fountainhead.

After, when we do receive the new knowledge, it becomes whole and logically connected. All learning has momentary confusion, while the old knowledge is broken down and the new is incorporated. After this synthesis occurs, closed cycles and logic begin again until the next "stroke of inspiration," **DMP**, (or "genius",) come along. In the meantime, perhaps we can assist this process by learning the principles of learning to be ready for the next burst of learning or "breakthrough." A little more *metacognition* might help. Learning about learning is worthwhile.

POSITIVE, NEGATIVE, NEUTRAL
APPROACHES TO LEARNING

The method one chooses to use in incorporating new knowledge reveals an important concept in learning. The universal principle will work if allowed to do so, by the right application of what we already know. Methods of learning, acceptance of, or proving new ideas can greatly influence the learning rate. It can also set direction and restrict learning to specific areas. Given three persons somehow endowed with equal amounts of knowledge, if they follow differing approaches to learning, the amount and direction of learning may be different in each person. It is not what you know but who you know, if the who is yourself.

Those using the **positive approach** assume everything is true, until it is experienced as untrue. Every new idea is theoretically accepted as truth, until application of it shows it as false. Those using the **negative approach** assume everything is untrue, until proven to be true. In the third approach or **neutral approach**, neither assumption is made, but the new idea is held suspended until it is observed to be true or false. (This is known as the scientific method of learning).

History is replete with examples of the first two methods of learning. Indeed, as history progresses they come into conflict one with another. Although there have been many cultures represented in history, our records of all of them are incomplete. Many have become extinct except for their relics at archaeological diggings. The surviving records have produced two philosophies which have dominated western thought. These two philosophies which typify the two approaches to learning are the Judaic-Christian culture and the Greco-Roman culture. The Judaic-Christian culture used the positive approach to learning, and the Greco-Roman culture used the negative approach. It can be debated which of these two cultures conquered the most minds. But we find both methods of approach in modern thought.

The two following idea lists is a comparison of the two methods:

JUDAIC-CHRISTIAN	GRECO-ROMAN
1. Ideas, figments, notions	1. Ideas, figments, notions
2. Believe true until experienced false	2. Believe false until proven true
3. Faith/Belief	3. Reason
4, Action on belief	4. No Action till Proof
5. Ideal of little children in learning and believing	5. Nature and disposition of the philosopher extolled
6. Future-oriented, looking ahead positively; prophesy archetype in thinking	6. Historically directed, gaining direction from records; retrospective thought
7. Intuitive source of ideas empirically confirmed	7. Empirical source of ideas proved by mental conclusion
8. Spiritually and religiously imbued thinking	8. Logic as the basis of thinking

The disputes between these two approaches to learning has led to another method, the scientific method. It is an answer to the incompatibility and shows an impartiality, that is neutral toward the possible moral issues underlying the two approaches of the positive and the negative.

In the scientific method or **neutral approach**, the conclusive test of new knowledge is observation. If events are not observable then they are not subject to scientific research. The next requirement of this approach is that the phenomena must be repeatable and demonstrable to others, when the same conditions are present. The special problem of applying the scientific method to the study of the future, is that the future is not repeatable. The future is beyond the senses and therefore observation is impossible. Because of these obstacles in the neutral approach, the future as a general subject in science is largely ignored, with the exception to some futuristic trends of research.

Unfortunately, the schools also neglect the topic of the future because of the influence of hard science. History and its many divisions finds place in every curriculum, but even the known elements of the future are sadly neglected. Except for momentary speculative digressions, our schools perpetuate the attitudes of history. That is not mentioning the long range political agendas inherent in public education.

The future may be considered as all knowledge, we have not yet learned. (It is this feature that makes Futurlogics a research method.) If this conception is carried to its logical conclusion, we connect the following theory to learning approaches. *How we learn and how we use "present knowledge" determines what we will see in the future.* Whether a teacher sees a future or not has no bearing, for what the child learns is what the child will use to face the future. If the teacher has no conception of the future then he prepares his students blindly. Every teacher should have some conception of the results of his teaching or he teaches with no purpose. Students must know why they are in school.

In Futurlogics, all the learning approaches are needed: the positive, the negative, and the neutral approaches of the scientific methods. However, emphasis will be placed with the positive approach as it is under-played in present educational procedures. Favoring any single approach will cause a narrow view, but to counter-balance the existing trends, stressing the positive approach is necessary until balance is achieved. Need for balance suggests that all methods assist us to learn.

By definition, the positive approach accepts all new knowledge equally with present knowledge. No restrictive or inhibitive effect is seen with present knowledge upon newly-learned ideas.

The negative approach suggest that existing knowledge is best and new ideas are admitted only after passing a test. This certification by proof implies lesser value of the new, and sets up a block between the new and the old.

The scientific method accepts nothing until it is certified by objective proof and/or peer review. Things not seen may not be admitted to exist.

Other methods or approaches which may be blends of the three named threads of thoughts are not addressed as they will be found to be effectively positive, negative or neutral anyway.

All methods define the acceptance of new knowledge relative to old knowledge. Again this says, that present accepted knowledge obstruct new knowledge, or the method will assist learning the new knowledge.

There are impossibilities and impossibilities. When one undertakes to expose a "false impossibility" the effort will inspire the mind to find ways to do the impossible. Nothing will elevate the mind to do more than it has done than to know that what was once impossible, is now assuredly possible. It takes a moment of insanity to learn new truths, that were once not even thought of, or were thought to be "impossible." Creative thinking will expose theses 'impossibilities' for what they are and make possible the designs and plans of man. Look for the controversial, metaphoric, and the impossible to begin the brain storm, and creativity will follow. Accept nothing as impossible at first and more likely than not, this will be a self-fulfilling prophecy. This is why the study of futurlogics will induce creativity, because it is commonly accepted that *the future is impossible to foresee.* Is learning the future really impossible? It can be shown that our attitude toward the future may have more impact upon our success than our past performances do.

Chapter III

CYCLES AND MODES

HOLISTIC THINKING
FACTIONAL THINKING
FRACTIONAL THINKING

Sometimes a subject is best understood when contrasted against its opposite. **DMP** is such a subject. But what is its opposite? We are unable to see the future, we don't hear the future, we don't touch things of the future, and we can't smell or taste what has not occurred. We are unable to remember what has not yet happened. Any thinking that contains the operation of the memory, senses, reflection, judgment, creativity, patterned, in exclusion of other ways of thinking, that is beyond the limits of a pure mental grasp is a cycle. **DMP** is cycle free thinking. **DMP** is HOLISTIC THINKING.

A cycle is thought which uses any of the observational channels of the senses or processes of memory etc.. Seeing is believing and observation is experience. If we see what we believe or think about what we see, then we are using a cycle, that is the see-think cycle. If we think about what we remember, and remember what we think about, we are cycling namely the think-know cycle. In fact, the scientific method uses cycles of observation and thought. Philosophy is based upon the cycles of logic and reason. (Note: In a philosophical discussion it is not sufficient to say that an object exists simply because one sees it. There must be logical proof that it exists. In such a style of thinking certain methods of learning are excluded, masked, filtered to enhance the use of others. i.e., reason and logic, and the purpose of philosophy is to use these methods only, to think and to attain knowledge.)

When a learning approach based upon a cycle is used to the exclusion of the other means of learning it becomes a *mode of approach* or simply a **mode**. Total learning is **DMP** where all the mind is used to intuitively arrive at knowledge. A mode is an approach to learning where only a portion of the mind's process is used to arrive at knowledge. **DMP** is Cycle free and Mode free thinking.

Cycles and modes are not as strange a definition as it might seem. Cycles are a common part of thought. When we concentrate on something to exclude extraneous thoughts, we produce a cycle. We want to focus on every possible aspect. Don't we close our eyes to hear and concentrate better? Don't we study where we will not be distracted? Cycles are problems only when we try to learn the future with them, or attempt to think creatively, or when we learn something new.

How often do we ignore an idea that pops into the mind because it does not fit into our box of knowledge? Because we are trying to pay attention to a particular subject of thought or a particular object of perception, we cast our thoughts away from new or different ideas. Many inventions and discoveries have come from the accidental and 'illogical' or seemly intrusive thought. Seldom does the new knowledge at which we marvel, come from the logical effect. We must pay attention to the new ideas that apparently burst into our consciousness, seemingly at the wrong time. New ideas seem to break focus.

Once in a while we have to suspend logic and allow a voice to these new ideas. Logic is important and indispensable to clear thinking, but it should not dominate learning. It has a time and a place. Logic is the rule of thought we use to maintain a cycle that so often eludes **DMP** of intuition. There is a time to focus, and there is other times we must scan and splay our thoughts, to gain vistas and the big picture.

We will always have to use what we already know to learn new things. This is especially true of learning of the future. Using what we already know to discover and describe the future employs the principles of parameter, simile, metaphor, parable, types, allegories, analogy, comparison, etc., to approach the future. Using what we have learned through a cycle causes the modal effect, and what we know interferes with what we will yet learn. Cycles, modes and models should be viewed as tools to produce, not the finished product.

BASIC MODES

Looking at the future in the light of the see-think and the think-know cycles gives our research a new perspective, if not a new meaning. Our notion, beliefs, perceptions and knowledge obtained through a cycle, or limited approach to learning, can affect the way (and the things) which we can learn about the future. It can prevent us from from thinking clearly about the things that have not happened yet. When knowledge gained from a cycle is used as a base to further research the future, it is called a mode, which is simply a shortened form of "mode of approach." Simultaneously, mode means the knowledge gained from cycle thinking and it means the knowledge gained from the same cycle used to study the future. It is the bank of knowledge used as a base to study and describe the unknown elements of the future. A mode can be thought of as the perspective of the future as viewed through a particular cycle of a learning technique. Modes hide information as it focuses information.

Since modes derive from cycles and cycles are the limited use of the mind and its processes, modes essentially limit the intuitive learning, or **DMP**. If we do not know the origin of our knowledge, we cannot think clearly. Tracing to the source of what we know and how we came to know it, is fundamental to **DMP**. Futurlogics requires that we be able to look back and see how we came to know anything we use, as data or information to research the future. Futurlogics goes beyond the *game rules* of cycles and modes. Basically we must/should seek origins.

We must ask ourselves to discern the cycle: did we learn this from observation, authority, reason, hearsay, imagination, insight, or some other source? Knowing when an idea first entered the mind and the circumstances surrounding it, can help develop **DMP**.

Not knowing which cycle we have come from, we fall victim to interpreting everything from a narrow perspective. Science alone is not enough. Religion, philosophy, or history alone are not enough. Any narrow approach to learning, that excludes other ways of learning, is not enough. We must adopt an overall approach, understanding how we learn is not more important than the knowledge we learn itself. *The end must not be frustrated by the means.* In Futurlogics the end justifies the means. Heuristics finds its employ here. Or, use whatever works to get the job done.

All modes of learning, all methods of science, religion, philosophy, history, psychology, imagination, experience, art, music, etc.. Insight, intuition and the total mind must be used to study the future.

MODES AS MENTAL BLOCKS

We have moments when our mind fails to serve us well—those annoying occasions in which we can't remember something, or else we can't keep our mind "on it." Something distracts us or we are occupied with worries. The common, everyday "mental block" has special interest because this annoyance is similar to the subtler workings of the mode.

Simplistically, we could say that the mode is a mild mental block. However, instead of preventing some thought or idea to surface to consciousness, the mode will only distort the thought to conform to the thought pattern it uses. These distortions, though slight, will have an accumulative effect. When this effect is present in any learning method we have the modal effect.

Modes are not new. We hear that we should be objective in dealings and avoid the subjective approach. Personal feelings, emotions, and opinions sometimes prevent us from seeing things as they really are. We commonly seek counselors to help us make objective decisions. (There is nothing inherently wrong with being subjective with reality, if it is done with balance and interplay.) To be completely objective is to be thoughtless. If there were not opinions, creeds, philosophies, hopes— then living would be sterile. We should be subjectively objective and objectively subjective, to think clearest.

No human knows everything, and complete objectivity is impossible. We have to fill in the missing parts of reality with our own subjective input. As living thinking beings, "how we think" influences "what we think." Modes are a manner of thinking that influences what we think in a predictable way. Defining the term mode again we can say:

❐ 1.   The mode is somewhere between the solid hard core prejudice and the mild predisposition. When we engage in the study of Futurlogics, we will use this concept of the mode. We want to avoid the effect of "old knowledge," either preventing the learning of "new knowledge," or somehow *coloring* it, so much so that, true understanding is not achieved. Futurlogics, then is a way of being as objective about the future as possible—realizing that the future is not within the objective range of the senses, and that the subjective faculties of the mind must be used through a special technique.

❐ 2.   A mode is only a mode when we are swallowed up in it. If we are conscious that we are in a mode, then we can take measures to prevent the effect of such a narrow perspective, upon thinking and learning. Part of Futurlogics aim is to become conscious of the various modes that we use, so clear and open-minded thought can take place. Then the intuitive learning of **DMP** is possible.

❐ 3. Modes are approaches to learning where the old existing knowledge overlays a pattern or "coloring," to the new knowledge acquired by that pattern, or cycle. We know of open-minded and closed-minded personalities, a mode is a compartmentalized version of closed-minded thought, except that it does not concern itself with life in general. Closed-mindedness is like looking at the world through a knothole. A mode is like looking at the future through a keyhole.

Learning through **DMP** is a completely block free means of learning. **DMP** is the ideal of learning.

SIX MODES IN FUTURLOGICS

In beginning a study of the future it would seem we have limitless starting points. Not all of these will develop into a mode. The possible attitudes, opinions, frames of mind, and definitions, subject to the concept of modality, eventually limit themselves. But man, being a creature of habit and economy, will settle on favorite cycles, which will feedback into themselves and generate the modes, we have discussed. Since we have common personality traits with similar motivations and common experiences, there are common grounds from which modes spawn, and it is because of this fact that special or dominant modes persist.   There are six major modes which are common modal approaches to the future.

Imagine looking through a kaleidoscope—every time we move it, it changes. There is an infinite variety to its color and designs. But when we take the kaleidoscope apart, we discover that there are just a few pieces of colored glass, a diffusing medium to destroy fine detail and enhance general form, and a tube to direct the line of vision to the mirrors. The cycle mode concept, though infinite in variation, is similarly simple. Only six basic modes appear when we take things apart and "look under the hood."

Each of the modes common to thinking about the future must be investigated individually. As we do this we can know when we are thinking in a particular mode. When we can be conscious that we are in a mode, it becomes easy to use **DMP** and the system of Futurlogics. First we analyze the modes then we synthesize them. It is subjective thought producing complete objectivity. **DMP** is mode and cycle free thinking.

THE ANALYSIS OF THE SIX MODES

Modes are not only a method of learning, they are also the knowledge produced by a cycle used in the mode. Each one of these six modes produce a conception of the future, with characteristics drawn from the various cycles and knowledge derived through the mode. The six modes will be referred to interchangeably as follows:

- Retrospective mode..............Absolute future
- Observational mode..............Natural future
- Imaginary mode....................Imaginary future
- Assumptive mode..................Artificial future
- Creative mode.......................Synthetic future
- Model mode..........................Paradigm future

For example the Artificial future is the "future" "seen" through the assumptive mode. This is true respectively for the other "futures" as seen through their modes.

Futurlogics takes the above modes and puts them to special use, in a systematized mental process developed, as a learning ground for **DMP**. But, we must first learn the separate modes of approach to the future, before we can synthesize them, in the system called Futurlogics.

When we can use all the above modes separately, then simultaneously, by using Futurlogics, we can achieve **DMP** (**D**irect **M**ind **P**erception; **D**irect **M**ental **P**rocess). But the modes should be learned first as separate components. They should not only be understood, but they must be used. They then, take on the role of a model of thought or a "future."

Someday we will have to stand on our own and be accountable for everything we have been taught. As we learn to drive an automobile we realize that eventually we would have take our first solo drive. Futurlogics should likewise train its students to go out on their own eventually. Futurlogics demands we become self-reliant, self-taught.

Before we arrive at the time, when we are able to leave our teachers behind and learn on our own, we will have to learn the system. When all the Futurlogics modes are learned and used interchangeably and alternately so that they become a multi-faceted view of the future, then we are ready to fully understand Futurlogics and **DMP,** as a mental system to "see" what lies ahead.

The mode is a thought routine. How can you get out of a rut or unproductive routine? This part may be skipped till after reading the next section on the methods. It is included in this book as an insert for those having difficulty "flipping paradigms," or changing modes as required in the futurlogics method of seeing the future through six perspectives. But if you want a small diversion, the following list below is offered as a suggestion:

1. Vary some element in the "pool."
   (Pool is the focus and the vista of consciousness. Consciousness can be thought of as analogous to the eye. There is macular consciousness and peripheral consciousness. This is the pool.)
   a. Get a big picture or vista of the routine.
   b. See the routine as a model of some larger view.
   c. Determine what is variable and what is immutable.
   d. Make the immutable vary and fix the variable to a constant.
2. Follow some ridiculous 'soot organon'.
   (**Soot** is black carbon residue that covers everything after a fire. This is the residue of enthusiasm which is the original fire of zeal that has since gone out.
   Organon is the system of rules and principles considered as an instrument of guidance as of knowledge or thought.)

a. In everything there are unknowns that are given names to cover
ignorance and provide a quick reference, bring to the light of
scrutiny the true origins of these ornate names. Start with the
obviously ridiculous and work towards the subtle sublime names.
b. Essentially uncover the ignorance or avoidance of ignorance by
drilling through the nomenclature that covers reality. Go from
academia to common sense.
3. Change subject return.
a. Reverse the outcome of the routine. If it is productive then make it
diminish the return as the efficiency increases. Demonstrate how going
to school makes one more susceptible to propaganda and deception.
b. 'Ignorance is bliss' to 'Ignorance will be painful'. 'Knowledge is
power' to 'knowledge is debilitating.'
4. Think about things in a different mood.
a. Of course emotions melt logic and soften the hard reality. Or emotions
make the difficult hard and intractable.
b. Realize some will be clinicians others will be activists. And there
exist a spectrum in between.
5. Get additional data or points of view.
a. Stop and look around. Step back and view from another point of view.
Look at the competition and imagine how the enemy looks at you.
Or see this situation from your enemies eyes.
b. See back at the subject as if from out of the box. Get back at
point of inception.
c. Review the origin and trace the genesis of the routine.
6. Prove or put under some mental process such as showing to be funny as
worthless.
a. Change your logic such as moving to another futurlogical mode.
b. Realize that logic is memorized rules of thought. Change the rules
and the logic. Set up some de Morgans theorem to normalize.
(de Morgans theorem is a transforming postulate of logic.

$$\overline{(A + B)} = \overline{A} * \overline{B} \text{ and } \overline{(A * B)} = A + B$$

or in words

Not (A or B) equals not A and not B
Not (A and B) equals not A or not B

)
Many rules can be redefined to effect the same result.
Logic was defined from and model for those whose vision of the big
picture is lacking. If your map or model is enhanced then refine
the logical relations along with the remodeling.
c. Everything has comedy in it.
7. Leave some part out.
a. See how long the routine lives with missing organs and functions.
b. learn to use denial and defiance as a tool of analysis rather than
to cover up an unwanted realization.
8. Put a known fact instead of an unknown.
a. Substitute a perfect replacement to a problem area
b. Replace what is perfect with the worst possible case.
c. Destructive testing should be conducted to determine the viability of
the routine, to see if it will run out of the rut.
9. Predict the future of the routine or rut.
a. Prediction, foretelling, prophesy will give perspective to any study.
Then start at item one and recycle to this point again. This should
create the expanding spiral to break out of the routine/mode.

PART TWO

METHODS

REMARKS ON THE MODES

Temporal knowledge, crossing time, generally speaking can be divided into three categories: knowledge of the past, knowledge of the present, and knowledge of the future. History, knowledge, and foreknowledge constitute the experience which we have—with the temporal environment of time. Experience with all three gives contact with reality in all of its phases. The fourth category would be knowledge of knowledge, which is recursive and is not time based but is mind based. Generally speaking again, this fourth category of knowledge can be over three domains again: imagination, certainty and creativity.

Sometimes, we are found to be specialized in the past or the present. When we are overweighted in one area (such as history), the self-sustaining effect of cycles causes us to interpret the other areas of the temporal environment by **it**. If we are overeducated in history, we try to describe the present and the future in terms of that history. There is no problem with this, if it is done with balance, realizing that if we channel all approaches through one of these specialized banks of information— we produce a mode.

The six Futurlogics modes are generated through this type of specialization. Since it is important to use all phases of knowledge, history, present scanning and foreknowledge to approach the future, we will investigate each method separately so we can improve them and use them in balance. Know when to specialize and/or when to generalize.

In the chapter on the **ABSOLUTE FUTURE**, the cycle of retrospection is used to approach the future, and the role of interpreting the future in the pattern of the past/history is covered. The organic origin of the absolute future is our memory.

In the chapter on the **NATURAL FUTURE**, as the observational mode describes it, is seen in terms of present knowledge of observation. The organic origin of the natural future is our senses.

In the chapter on the **IMAGINARY FUTURE**, we see the power of imagination and how the imaginative cycle becomes a mode. The organic origin of the imaginary future is our ability, to mentaly reflect with our imagination.

In the chapter on the **ARTIFICIAL FUTURE** we learn of a future assumed or judged to facilitate action or thought. We learn how assumptions are taken subconsciously even unconsciously. The organic origin of the artificial future is, our ability to emotionally assume to further action or thought.

In the chapter on the **SYNTHETIC FUTURE** the creative cycle is studied. Man's power to create is seen as a modal dimension of the future. The organic origin of the synthetic future is our ability to create an make with our mind and hands.

In the chapter on the **PARADIGM FUTURE** it shows how the amount of foreknowledge we already possess is used, to model and prototype the future. We discuss the problems and advantages, in trying to interpret the future through this mode, and we learn how the paradigm mode can be both a model and a modal approach to the future. Conscious-knowledge is the organic source of this mode.

In these chapters, the terms cycles, mode, and future sometime will be used (seemingly) interchangeably. The essential distinctions to be recognized, when an exact definition is required, is this:

a *cycle* is a learning technique using only a portion of the mind and the senses and is repetitive;

a *mode* is a theorizing technique where the world, as it applies to this book—the future—is interpreted through the medium of a particular cycle or cycles. As the fugue is to music, the mode is to thought.

The word *future* is used interchangeably between the mental concept of the future or mental model, and the actual future.

Mode and future are sometimes used interchangeably. A conception of the future that is derived through the observational mode— or the natural future—is so much like that very system of learning the future, that it is essentially a mode still. This is true of each of the six individual futures. Each can be termed as a mode, if it is stressed that it is not the actual future but a conception of the future. Modes then use the peepholes of cycles to perceive the whole world, or universe, as it were.

Chapter IV

ABSOLUTE FUTURE

THE PAST IS PROLOGUE

Our memory ties us to the past, and we find continuity with the present. Indeed, we gain the meaning of things from their histories. No one will argue that studying the past will help us deal better with the present. History gives us a sense of direction and points our minds toward the right course as we look to the future. The function of history is an essential part of our dealings with the environment, especially the environment of time. (Memory is the organic source of this mode.)

To understand the retrospective cycle of using the past to discover the future, we must understand clearly the nature and characteristics and definition of the past.

First the past can never be changed. It can only be discovered and recorded. Sometimes, the revisions and changes we see in some accounts of history, gives us the feeling that the past has changed, but this is due to the fact that history is not the past, and that records of the past were unevenly kept. Some ancient civilizations had extensive records that have survived to the present, while others just as extensive, were destroyed by war and conquerors if not natural disasters. Some civilizations have left behind records that have not yet been deciphered or translated. When these records are translated, new history is added to the existing bank of knowledge. Variations in recording may give the illusion that the past changes—but the past does not change. Only our knowledge of the past changes. History changes with new discoveries.

The fact that the past cannot be changed makes it conveniently constant and linear. There is only one true history of the past. This simplicity gives us a criteria by which we can discern between differing historical accounts of the same period. We logically conclude that we must end up with only one true history of the past.

The past's singularity and immutability suggests the word absolute, and this property leads us to name this future Absolute, as it is the future seen by the lens of the retrospective cycle. This view of the future through the eyes of the past tends to attribute to it characteristics of the past. The ABSOLUTE FUTURE then, is the future seen from the perspective of the past. It is the future seen from the mirrors of the past.

Such concepts of the future have emerged in the course of history only under other names. We see in ancient Greece a similar future—instead of calling it absolute, they called it Fate. The Fates were a mythological group composed of three goddesses who were given the power to decide human destiny. Their names were Clothe, Chachesis, and Atropos; these three determined the beginning, length, and end of people's lives respectively. The theory that the Fates arranged the lives of each person caused great concern among the philosophers, as they could not come up with a better explanation in the face of life's vicissitudes. Many of the Greek plays express these feelings of frustration, because Greek philosophy could not deal with the future. Themes in their plays were designed to portray the uselessness of going against the designs of the Fates.

Myths reflect the attitudes of a culture. They are not products of the culture. The myths would have died, if they did not explain things better than the philosophers. In all of the philosophical thinking of that era, the future was the subject least discussed because they lacked the mental tools to deal with it. In fact, there is no philosophy today concerning the future.

In these mythological explanations of time and temporal conditions, the Greeks had multiple gods and deities that caused a singular linear future. This singular future was Fate. Fate was like history: it must be resigned to completely by submission. It is just accepted.

Among the ancient cultures, the Hebrew culture was distinctive because it worshiped a singular God who provided His people with a diverse and plural future. There were many mansions in their heavens. Instead of a singular future they had a plural future or future(s). Even their prophesies depended upon the moral climate of the people. If they repented, they could change the whole outlook of their future. The plural future of the Hebrews was encouraged as it furthered focused responsibility upon the people to live the law. It engendered individual responsibility for their choices. The person was faced with sin if he did not make a good decision or choice.

The Hebrews had "one God" and many rewards in the heaven(s) of their afterlife. Their future was contingent upon righteousness. The Greeks, however, had "many gods" but only one singular future called fate. Moral responsibility should be based upon other contingencies that were not individually controllable. With a singular future what they did made no difference to the final outcome of their prearranged destiny and moral rectitude was not stimulated. No personal responsibility for their future has had very sad outcomes with great civilizations.

THE PLURAL FUTURE VS. THE SINGULAR FUTURE

We could visualize the future as many possibilities funneling down through the present to end up as the past—the neck of the funnel is the present. There are no possibilities in the past. Only absolute fact and singularity characterizes what passes the present to the past. But, if we move the funnel of the present, as it were, into the future so that we look at the past of the future behind the funnel as if it were the past, we produce a singular future, at least to the new position of the neck. Analogically, this is essentially what the retrospective mode does, and the absolute future, in turn, is the future from the imaginary funnel back to the present as it were.

Use of history exclusively to view the future produces the same effect. Looking at the future through the lens of the past will tempt us to see the future as singular. But, the facts are that we are alive and able to make an impact upon our environment. Everything we do can change the future to some degree, according to the power and resources within our grasp.   If we choose, we have the power available to blow the surface of the planet to dust. Facts and experience compel us to look at our future as plural. A plural future requires us to look forward with responsibility and creativity. If we tend to avoid responsibility, we may want to view the future as a singular thing beyond our control, thus alleviating culpability in how everything turns out.   Nevertheless, the greater the power our knowledge gives over our environment, the more plural the future must be envisioned. If our will is empowered with knowledge that enables us to plan and design the future as we elect, at least within reasonable limits, we tend to pluralize the future if we choose, or restrict it. if we also choose.

A plural future offers choice, whereas the singular future of the absolute mode restricts volition. Strict adherence to the retrospective mode of approaching the future produces a singular future that paralyzes our will and freedom of choice.

SECURITY VS. FREEDOM

If the singular future of the retrospective mode restricts volition. Why do we tend to use it to approach the future? Obviously, we desire certainty. Certainty is required in a world in constant flux. Also, security is next in line of desirability. Without a sure base, we hesitate to act. We trust the past because it does not change. We find the past to be a linear unchangeable part of our temporal environment. The past is safe. There is the temptation to believe that if we are to make the future safe and certain, we will have to make it like the past. Thus we concede to this mode to feel safe.

The singular and invariable future of the absolute mode is a lure to false security. In the business of staying alive, happy and healthy, any uncertainty is seen as a threat. Sudden departures into the realms of uncertainty can result in anything, even death. The desire to base action upon certainty and safety, persuades us to believe the absolute future. Unwittingly we reject the more plural future, for the sense of security that a strict historical perspective of the future can lend.

THE PROBLEM OF FREEDOM

Security without freedom is a prison. It will take captive our creativity also. In order to be free to live in the whole world, we should be able to move in it as we desire. The linear singular future gives a chart and a bearing that cannot be improvised by a change of mind. It is a map with no detours. Freedom runs a head-on collision course with the absolute future. The retrospective view and its historical perspective should be resolved, before a sound understanding of the true future or future(s) can be reached.

Let us consider the problem of freedom as the self-concept in this mode is brought to the fore. Using a short range future as given, we look ahead to the next two days. Doing this, we see it in an abridged form or our freedom of volition will be threatened. Theoretically, this could go on until everything is decided. We would see a vicious cycle, and awareness of our own decisions and choices in advance. But can we foresee our own thoughts before we think them? If we can, then when the time arrives that we have foreseen, we say, "I have already decided this," remembering the preview of the future we have had. Decision becomes only a memory recall, of seeing ourselves making the decisions in the first place. We can imagine that the constant remembering of previous decisions would be like a series of infinite "deja vu" experiences, looking at ourselves between two mirrors, seeing a chain of images. Taken to its extreme limits, we can also imagine that if we were somehow to see all our lives before us, we would never have to think again, having made thought a matter of remembering.

But knowledge gained from the future becomes knowledge to change the future; and it is fuel to the engine of free will. The self-image in the retrospective mode is the most frustrating part of this approach, to the future and the environment. It seems to defy our very thoughts. If we use it, we find our volitive powers swallowed up, for in this version experiences, thoughts, and even our own will is seen as a historical fact.

ELIMINATING SELF HELPS THE MODE TO WORK

Since conflict and anxiety are created when we see ourselves in the future through the absolute mode, the best way to use the retrospective cycle will be to avoid the self and things related to volition. A short discussion of the common ways to avoid self and make this mode work, will help develop understanding, of the absolute mode and some techniques we can employ. Although any method, that in some way attenuates the self could be a technique, only the more obvious will be treated:

If we look at the future in the same way an astronomer looks into the heavens, the self is diminished the same way that our planet becomes a small speck in the galaxy. Everything in the universe is in galactic dimensions, not only diminishing the earth, but dwindling man. Therefore, anything that man does will not be of any moment compared to the explosive energy of the birth and death of a star. So also, if the future is conceived in galactic terms, then the self is insignificant in the whole scheme of things. We see immediately that this technique does not work with the close in problems of daily living.

Just as common is the consideration of events beyond the span of our lives. This way we naturally eliminate problems encountered with seeing ourselves—erasing ourselves by death in the future. Most of us find that a preoccupation with things that will transpire after our demise, is a very heavy and sobering subject, so much so that this kind of afterlife preoccupation is commonly within the realms of religion. But when the deep future is studied with a belief in a life after death, then the problem of seeing the self in the future is again renewed. Many refuse to consider the assertions of religions because they enliven the conflict of self and freedom in these afterlife concepts. Therefore, some religions are seen as a battleground of free will and free agency. The altruistic behavior found in most religions with a self-effacing manner of interpreting things, typify this reaction to the freedom problem.

When the absolute mode fails, it is because it does not provide for self and freedom and adaptation to new conditions. We become a fish out of water.

The next means of avoiding the self in the absolute future uses the concept of destiny. Although similar to the "beyond life method" there is a slight difference. The "destination" method of avoiding the self conflict does so, by not considering the immediate vicissitudes of life, but rather by centering the view of the future towards the final outcome. Although similar to the technique of eliminating the time of our life span, concept of destiny ignores the time of immediate concern. This is like saying that since Tuesday is not as important as Monday, we will think of Wednesday. The concept of destiny keeps the self at enough distance, so that the conflict of self and decision for the future are avoided.

Rather than avoid the self in the absolute future, we should find a system that allows us to see the self and all decisions with none of the concomitant problems. The absolute mode would produce less anxiety and restriction if we could resolve the three selves we contain: our past self, our present self, and our future(s) selves. Futurlogics offers a relief to the problems encountered by use of the retrospective cycle and the absolute mode.

The self is important since our survival and progress is linked to its expression. The exercise of free choice should be spontaneous and creative. To rely only on one way to view the future will not provide this latitude and range. Maximum volition is essential to progress or success. We resist others telling us how to live, and looking ahead in the absolute mode provokes the problems of freedom. Unless we know there are other ways of learning about the future, we will resent that future self imagined through the absolute mode.

A phenomena seen in the self-improvement books currently popular is reminiscent of these concepts. These books suggest that if one imagines oneself as already achieving the goal, or the desired objective, or even rehearsing the accomplishment of the goal mentally, the mind will work as if it were already done. We know that without a future, our motivation goes nowhere. Changing one's future changes the expression of our whole motivational system. Therefore, this trick upon the motivational system uses the imagined self to commit to a future to motivate us. If we can get our imagined self to commit to a future goal, then naturally this commitment presupposes the present self as already committed to that goal. Thus, we are motivated indirectly. Sometimes we imagine an after-this-time-self to make the absolute mode work, as this force of "tradition" constrains the true self, we make an imagined self to distract this modal force or restriction.

The future is our goal and the self of that future is the identity we will eventually become. We are motivated toward our goals and our goals motivate us to achieve them. We relate to the future, and our assumptions of the future have a great deal to do with how we live. We could investigate this further, but we cannot do this without a basis of comparison. We must learn the other modes to have a platform for comparison. We must remake ourselves by looking ahead with a new identity.

DOES HISTORY REPEAT ITSELF?

"If you have seen it once, you will see it again!" It is said, "Studying history is the best way to find out what will happen in the future—because 'history repeats itself'." This prediction could be well and good if man did nothing differently than his ancestors, and did not progress. Accepting that man is essentially the same as his forefathers, in some areas is the shortcoming of seeing history as a prologue to the future. There are areas where we differ greatly from those who lived before us. We need only reflect upon the date the first atomic bomb was detonated. In the light of that explosion, we should have seen a whole new world ahead. History repeats itself only, if man does not progress or change. However, for centuries this form of approaching the future has sufficed. It has become ingrained in our culture, and we almost unconsciously view the future through the eyes of our ancestors. Once this view is recognized as a perspective of the future from the retrospective cycle, it can be revealed as a mode. Although we can not completely escape the use of history to determine the future, we want to use it according to the right mix, to properly extrapolate the past to futurity. We want the historical approach to be a tool of Futurlogics, not the total method of prediction.

An old gentlemen seeing the effects of inflation on his retirement said, "The future ain't what it used to be!" He expressed the need today to find a new way of approaching the future. Today there are no historical precedents. Worldwide communication, nuclear energy, the knowledge explosion, and computer data processing make obsolete a total reliance upon the retrospective view of the future. We must learn when to look to history and when to look through other ways.

Study Subjects for the Future-minded in the Absolute Future.

- *Parental Influences, Tradition, Inheritance.*
- *Social Memes or Viral Changes in Society.*
- *Educational Agendas.*
- *Economic Differences Impact i.e. "follow the money".*
- *Social Pressures, Conformity, Individuality.*
- *Language Patterns, Communications role in change mechanics.*
- *Group Thinking vs. Personal Thinking.*

Chapter V

NATURAL FUTURE

NATURAL FUTURE AS SEEN THROUGH
THE OBSERVATIONAL MODE

No one is as blind as the person who thinks he sees everything with his eyes. We sense such a small part of what is real, that it is doubtful that it represents even a sample of the total extent of existence. Dismissing the existence of anything because it is not observable emphasizes this form of blindness. There are other ways of learning and coming to know of things. Mental blindness is by far the most serious form, one for which there is often no cure. If, for some reason, we insist that everything be observable, then we lay ourselves open to a special form of blindness.

We previously explained a cycle by stating that a person tends to think about what he sees, and tends to see what he thinks about. Observation of things about us can cause this same cycle, in that we think about what we observe and observe what we think about. If our observational powers only put us in touch with a small portion of reality, then we only think about them to a commensurate extent. We are forced to use only that portion of the mind that promotes or supports further observation.

If we attempt to learn about the world (and in the special case we are interested in the future) only through the powers of sense observation, we then find a limited and perhaps distorted view of things that the mode generates. Using the cycle of observation to learn about the future, we find the modal effects are also present. Whenever we realize how little we actually perceive through our senses, we can then appreciate the process of **DMP** and the Futurlogics system. The more we learn through intuition and insight the more we see the limitations of the senses. (The senses are the organic source of this mode.)

How much of the mind do we ignore? Scientist themselves state that the brain is capable of much more than is ever used. For them the last criteria of proof is that phenomena must be observable, and they set for themselves a limitation that cannot be overcome. One of the "phenomena" they will never observe is the operation of their own mind, and that is not observable except by the most private introspection. As long as science uses the mind to hypothesize, theorize, explore new frontiers of science, science will be limited by their lack of knowledge of the mind's role in observation and the senses themselves.

THE CONCEPT OF SELF IN THE OBSERVATIONAL MODE

One of the requirements of science is that all assertions must be either demonstrable or observable, by more than one person. When ever anything is proven, it is shown to all. Objectivity is stressed as personal input tends to invalidate the proof. Great care is taken to show that the finding is real and part of the environment, and not just the assertion of someone who wishes it to be real. Therefore peer review is a requirement.

Science studies nature, or it studies the nature of a particular thing. The natural future or the natural mode is that future seen through the eyes of those who depend solely upon the senses. Science sees the future through the observational mode, therefore the future seen, if other faculties of the mind are not used, is the Natural Future.

Science cannot study emotions or mental processes, since these are seen introspectively. Such things are behaviorally defined or externally visable parameters of the phenomena are used to measure the emotion and mental activities. Therefore, what kind of "self" does the observational mode see in the future? What is the concept of the "self"— if any—in the natural future? What manner of discernment is required to view the self and the introspected life?

In discussing the absolute mode, we came across the problem of seeing the self in the concept of the future viewed through the retrospective cycles. The question then naturally arises, what is the problems of seeing the self in the concept of the future viewed through the observational cycles? Our answer here is that the only parts of the self in the natural future seen, are the parts that are observable through the five senses. The self in this future sees itself as the reflection of his body in a mirror. Volition, decision, thought, or any introspectively known aspect of the self will not exist; they are not within the scope of the observational cycle. What is not seen does not exist in the pure application of this form of learning. The person seen through this mode is in mental suspension, not thinking, but only observing some external event. The strictest use of this mode then, makes the self exist without consciousness, unless it is the consciousness of observing.

THE PRESENT CAUSES THE FUTURE

What we now observe today was once the future of yesterday. Everything we see is the result of yesterday, and is seen as a logical effect of the causes we attribute to the happenings of the past. There seems to be a logical chain of events stretching from the past to the present and trending, if not extending into the future. We need to know where present things are going to predict the future. Simplistically, this is true "action in the present causes the future."

The sense organs put us into contact with nature. But, if we ignored other ways of dealing with reality and rely solely upon the senses, which form the channels of observation, we operate in the cycle which is the basis for this mode. One of the rules of unbiased observation is, the careful elimination of mental and emotional inputs into the process of observing. Observation is a form of non-thinking behavior—a mere data gathering activity in its best practiced form. Personal input of any kind is usually disdained as contaminating the report that a pure witness of events should produce. In order for the personal type of biasing to be canceled, two of the requirements of observation are: that there be an alternate witness and also that the phenomena is seen simultaneously by the second observer. It must be observable to all or the data is not reliable.

Observation can take place only in the present. We can see nothing of the past or the future with the physical organs of perceptions. Our view is restricted to the narrow band of time which is the present. We see only the beginning, or the middle, or the end, but we can never see them all at the same time.

Ongoing things are described in terms of cause, effect, and conditions. The observational mode must use this breakdown of events into parts, in order to use the logic that is correlative. The cycle between seeing and thinking produces strict rules of logic, prevalent in the observational methods of learning that typifies this approach. The study of science might be used as an example of the language and terms that the observational mode might be forced to use, if it is to be successfully applied to the future.

Concepts in this style of thinking cannot be true and untrue at the same time. When we look at things with other means such as **DMP**, which looks at the temporal environment all at once, a seeming contradiction can take place; a thing can be true and not true but at different times. Since the mind can hold the past, present and future all at once, truth and untruth may be experienced simultaneously. When we deal with the future and the time continuum of the environment with all the modes, we run contrary to the need to stress the requirement that things happen at the same time. Logic therefore is the bridge between past and future that gives need for memorizing cause and effect relationships. Further, logic ties all the moments of observation together so that they offer continuity to the flow of time. The observational mode fails without logic, because this method considers only the material environment of the present.

NATURAL FUTURE IS A
PROJECTION OF THE STATUS QUO

Children first learn through the things they observe. What we see then is, what we learn to expect. Explain to a child that, the temporary absence of his mother need not be a cause for concern! The inexperienced mind of the child sees only that his mother is not present. The natural extension of his thought convinces the child that the absence is permanent—he predicts only from what he sees—and he will not be convinced that she is soon to return, and there is no reason to cry. Simple observation tells the child that she is not there and there is no reason to believe she is soon to come back, unless there has been ample previous experience that the mother does return. If the child is trusting, the fear subsides, and the expectation of the mother's return supplants his fear, and soon he is playing with a toy.

Consider how many of us do the same thing? We judge the future by current conditions. If we say the future is just an extension of present circumstances then the modal effect is generated. We trust what we see until we learn to find other ways to trust in things unseen. Until we discern that there are things that eyes or ears have not seen or heard, we cannot extend our learning method beyond the observational mode.

By studying the future, the observational mode is put in its proper place, enhancing the future as one of those real things just beyond sense observation. Therefore, if one realizes that the future exists and it is extensive, then other means are sought. **DMP** is contrasted against this type of learning and it is a good approach to provide comparison.

PREDICTION BY GAUGING PERMANENCE

We know the stars assemble the atoms and the particles that make up the material environment. Everything in nature centers around the atom. There are a hundred different atoms (in actually there are more but their stability is in such short half-lives that we do not yet see their role in nature). In most cases, decay rates and conditions which accelerate decay are know. These regularities and rates of permanence allow us to project that such things will be found in the future.

Gold will always be gold, no matter where or when it is found. Though it is burnt, formed, blended, pounded, scattered, mined or recycled, it will always remain gold. It was there in the past and it will be there in the future. Likewise, the sun will always be a star and will follow the course of all stars as to birth, life and extinguishment. Knowing the conditions in which things happen and how long they exist, is the basis of prediction found in the scientific method. This is an excellent way of predicting and we do not detract at all from these techniques, but only stress that there are other ways which apply to the things with which science and observation cannot deal.

Touching the future by simple observation is good only in cases where a particular phenomena will endure a known time under given conditions, or is a direct result of cause and effect relationships. Knowing the permanence of matter in given conditions and possible potential events, typifies scientific predictions. The natural mode depends on the ability to observe and predict by logical process, and is very useful as long as we are aware of its limitations.

WE IMAGINE WE ARE SEEING THE FUTURE

In the observational mode a point in time must be imagined to be the present so we can "visualize" the future. This is a device we use to avoid the limitations of the senses. We are utilizing the minds eye to "see" the future. A **scenario** is nothing more than the power of imagination. By imaginary means we allow ourselves to believe we are seeing and observing, as if we were actually present and perceiving the future through our senses. We did this in the absolute mode by imagining the future has (already) happened and we are looking back to it. This technique for the natural mode is we imagine a point in the future as if it is now, and we are "there" looking around with our senses. This is one of such tricks of the imagination used to compensate for the limitations of certain cycles, used to predict the future.

A curious feature of the observational mode is found when we attempt to answer the question, "What happens to the period of time between the actual present and the imagined present?" The answer is that we cannot be conscious of that period of time, if we are using the purely observational mode. All things become an expanded present, so the time between the actual now and the imagined now cannot be realized unless, we *jump* (that is: *shift* as in "paradigm shift") into the use of another mode. Thus, it is impossible to consider the continuum of time (i.e., the temporal environment) when using the observational mode. It is characteristic of the observational mode that awareness is lost for this duration of time and its continuum. The consciousness of the actual past and future is lost also, because these things are beyond the senses. We are left with an expanded present—or a continuum of present only. The problem with the observational mode is, that it destroys our awareness of the flow of time from the past into the present and on towards the future. Using the observational mode excessively expands the present. This over emphasis is the reason, it can not be used solely to approach the future.

The imagination is used in all the modes. Indeed, if there were no imaginary content, thinking would be impossible. As we become more familiar with the imaginary mode we realize, how we subconsciously compensate for the inherent limitations of modes.

Study Subjects for the Future-minded in the Natural Future.

- *Professional Expertise,Specialization* effect/affect on *Observation.*
- *Life Span, Experience* role in thinking, learning, study.
- *Specialization of Occupations vs. the Generalist* in futuring.
- *Veracity of Data and Accuracy of Research, Trust.*
- *Peacetime Science vs. Wartime Science, Industry.*
- *Scientific Paradigm Distortion i.e. "Old School vs. New School."*
- *Unspoken Agendas in Science.*

Chapter VI

IMAGINARY FUTURE

IMAGINATION

Memory ties us to the past; our senses observe the present, but what mental process enables us to consider the future? Thoughtful imagination. Imagination is essential to prospective thought, suggesting that the analogy to the memory and sense observation may be the faculty of imagination. However, the power of imagination is essential not only to prospective thought, but to thought in general. We see this need immediately because we can imagine both the true and the false, the material and the immaterial with our minds eye. Imagination does more than enable the mind to view the future. (The mental ability to reflect is the organic source of this mode of approach to the future.)

No system of thinking can exist without the power of the imagination. All ideas of the future are in fact, displayed to our consciousness through the means of imagination. Through it we can construct symbols, the models and maps of the future. We rehearse mentally the outcome of the things we intend to do before they are actually done. Before performing each act we should first "do" it in our minds. Considering a dangerous circumstance, we suppose and draw plans and preparations before our first move. If we wish to cross a rushing river we first survey the river and then imagine possible ways of getting to the other side. We selectively eliminate the impractical from the potentially successful. We picture swimming, floating, ropes, rafts, or we glance to see if there is a narrow place up the river. An extremely long jump is immediately dismissed, but a log bridge is a possibility. Such a scenario of thought can take place in seconds. We course through the many possibilities in a chain of thought empowered by imagination. Through experience and judgment, we could settle upon a specific means to cross the river and we venture then to act.

The first large rivers must have been a major exercise in creativity for ancient man. Today getting across a busy city street may call upon the same spin of imagination. Although we do not have the same natural obstacles of yesteryears, there are synthetic obstacles inherent to modern civilization. Air travel, bridges, and ferries have solved the old river problem, but we have problems of tax, war, food production, overpopulation, the energy crunch and a host of other modern obstacles. The need for prospective imagination is obviously greater today than it has been previously. It would so seem, but in reality we are just as human facing challenges as our ancestors.

IMAGINE-THINK CYCLE

The cycles infer that we do not use all of the mind at once. There is a tendency to think about related things. Also, our perceptions and faculties are somewhat guided by our thoughts. This encompassing effect is no less true with the cycle of thought with imagination. We think about what we imagine and then we imagine things related to our thoughts. Our thoughts are then concentrated into what we have imagined and the cycle effect is generated. This is metacognition.

Brainstorming and free thinking exemplify the extreme examples of this form of thought cycling. There is no modal blocking with brainstorming when used to explore possibilities and consider probabilities; it liberates our creative ability through a free association of ideas, which is necessary to any futuristic thinking. But, if we forget the difference between the real and the imagined—we get the modal effect.

The mode of approach to the future where the imagination runs free is the imaginary mode. At one time it might have been called the "fantasy future" because this term connotes certain properties of the imaginary mode or future. But to stress the positive creative attributes, "imaginary future" was selected. A reverence and value to good thought process is very necessary at times, to penetrate areas that are considered unthinkable, to open the more difficult areas of the future. The future seen with this mode is as varied as the operations of the mind itself. Nevertheless, it does take on the underlying patterns that characterize the flights of fancy the imagination can take. To understand the imaginary future, if not the actual future, we must understand the imagination. Imagine if you will, the imagination in operation.

Such imaginative flights, if they are products of a particular mode, can be called a scenario; but in mode-free, cycle-free, logic-free thinking, they are called **DMP**. **DMP** has its own rules and the usual meaning of logic does not portray intuitive experience. Imagination is insight.

LOGIC AND IMAGINATION

The material origins of the natural future require a logic consistent with the properties of matter itself. This compensates for the modal distortion due to the control of a free run of the imagination. Most of the rules of science were invented, to make certain accepted discoveries explained things within the known material laws. It ensures these mechanics of logic separate fantasy, vain imaginations, and material reality.

Each mode has its own logic peculiar to the cycle that generates it. Also, if we were to invent a new mode, we would do it by organizing a set of rules for thinking, or logic to define the limits of imagination in the thinking process. Since each mode has its own logic, then each mode has its own scenario. In other words, the form of fantasized thoughts of the future is framed by the attitude of the mode. Modes are deductive in theme as the logics are confined to use a prescribe premise, to the exclusion of inputs from outside sources to the premise. Whereas, model thinking is inductive allowing input from outside sources, modal thinking is deductive allowing only input from the premise itself requiring that there must be a premise.

THE KNOWN AND THE UNKNOWN

The future may be said to consist of the known and the unknown, broadly speaking. The future generally is divided between the two, and it is in the unknown regions that the imagination can flourishes unfettered. The less we know, the more we imagine. Our imagination is always active, mainly because of the deficiencies in fact. The less we know of futurity, the more we imagine a future to fill in the blank spots. When we arrive at a point of knowledge, we have to leave behind our imaginary notions. The more we know of the future, the more we can know. But in the case of the imaginary mode, the less we know the more expansive the imaginary future becomes. The imaginary mode uses what is imagined to temporarily satisfy this need. But an imagined future is better than no future at all! Imagination is a wonderful tool, and being able to sift the real from the unreal is the key to ensures success. There is no need to imaginatively process settled knowledge unless that knowledge is specious. Counterfeit knowledge is undermining to the synergy of true discovery. The false reward of spurious knowledge is counterproductive to true imaginative research.

SEPARATING THE REAL FROM THE UNREAL

Learning to discern between the imaginary and the real is a lifelong struggle. We learn through hard lessons that fantasy is not a good basis for rash action. Very soon we will demand certainty and solidity before we act. Developing the ability to tell the difference between the imagined and the real, makes success and progress in this changing world possible. If there is difficulty separating the two, the imaginary mode generates. If we fail to clarify these twilight areas to avoid error, modal distortion is produced.

After all the modes are learned, it is by the power of our own imagination that we can synthesize them into one operation. With the imagination we can go from one mode to another, and avoid becoming dependent upon one narrow approach to the future. The mental grasp of the future **DMP** is made possible, when we have the imagination in control and we can trace to its origin any idea. If we can tell from where all ideas originate, we can then arrive at **DMP** and the control of imagination. On the other hand, without imagination there will be no **DMP** experiences.

FREE WILL, VOLITION, AGENCY

Free will is made possible through the powers of imagination. Also moral agency, if not morals themselves are possible only through the power of imagination. Without the ability to display to consciousness an alternative to the stimulus of the environment (emotions, drives, etc.), we would simply follow these impulses reflexively. Yet, by imagination we could fantasize being able to fulfill all our desires, wishes, goals, just by saying IF! Dreams ride on the wings of imagination. All consciousness is made possible with imagination, and without being aware of options, alternatives, possibilities, we can have no free will or volition. Indeed we would have no conscience. All cycles, logics, modes, and futures generated from them, restrict, guide or channel the imagination. Perfect free will is possible only when all the modes of approach are used to research the future, and we have a model or paradigm to organize our search and research of the future. This is Futurlogics. Thus when we refer to imagination in this theory, we define it as logic-free, cycle-free, mode-free thinking. Imagination is the engine of **DMP**. And again **DMP** is the contact with the future we can have in the views and scenarios we generate in our research.

Who can handle perfect freedom? Would we abuse it to our own destruction? Will we always need caretakers to limit us in our freedom for our own good? Many other questions arise when the imaginative powers are researched and implications discovered.

These ideas bring with them new freedom of the mind. If we are not used to thinking freely, we will feel a severe reaction. Generated responsibilities reach "critical mass" and a personal change will threaten old ideas and traditions. Many balk at the prospect of really thinking for oneself, yet those who love to explore frontiers will forge ahead excited by every new idea.

In the imagination one should be prepared and able, to use many different value systems to explore with the imagination. What we value will direct our thoughts more than thoughts, that do not connect to what we value. It is advisable to determine ahead, what is the priority of our system that gauges worth. Sincerity will allow very directed thought to goals that have some value. Also given we can suppose, and poise "givens," to enable us to extend our thoughts beyond the immediate. Being able to assign a value to an idea and apply it to the various conditions also assist one, in imaginative scenario generation.

What causes thinking? What causes thinking about thinking or metacognition? That is an even better question. But one answer is 'partial knowledge' causes thinking. Immediately, one might assume then that faith would squelch thinking as it is seen by some, as the training to accept 'partial knowledge' as the end, rather than the means to an end. Recognizing "what is partial knowledge" is key to thinking.

A know-it-all personality would follow as one not given to much thinking. The opposite is know-nothing-for-sure philosopher, whose technique to stimulate thought is to not take anything for granted. Perhaps the philosopher thinks too much with inadequate premise. Balance then comes to mind here, in a deliberation on the cause and productivity of thinking.

Faith is the ability to do the best with the least as is given in the futurlogics. Less is more as my German grandma instructed me, applies to the provocation of thought. This age now of information overhead and overload, tends to stun the thought process with too much data. Thinking then in the future will become the pursuit of meaning and relevance. With this definition then faith will be a great stimulus, to thought and thought about thought.

With Futurlogics the future, when known in part, can be provocative of thought that is, if one is not boggled by the vastness of the Future. The divisions of the future in the futurlogics then subdivide this vastness to sub-vastness where thought is provoked. To narrow down even further an aspect of the future and prompt actions, such as preparation and planning or scheduling. Although high emotions cause action generally of a temporary nature, safety and quiet following will cause much thought. This then resolves into experience. Thinking is using existing knowledge to leverage into greater knowledge, that will promote the activities relative to the future such as the planning and preparation. Also thinking will fill in the missing pieces of history when no documentation or artifact can enlighten.

Imagination is more important than knowledge ~ Albert Einstein

Study Subjects for the Future-minded in the Imaginary Future.

- *Academic Authority vs. the Self Evident.*
- *Inability to Handle the "Abstract Concepts."*
- *Administration of Resources or Influence of Money in Research.*
- *Acknowledgement of Originality vs. False Claims of Discovery.*
- *Mixed Metaphors or Hazards of the Never Ending Brain Storm.*
- *Differences in Individual Attitudes Towards Intuition/Insight.*
- *Mental Capacity to think of more than one thing at a time.*

Chapter VII

ARTIFICIAL FUTURE

THE ASSUMPTIVE MODE

What we have discussed so far has been in the arm chair of our own living room. We have not really come to terms with the real world. The needs and demands of material necessities force upon us another need for certainty. Life goes on regardless, and we often must live and act with inadequate knowledge of the actual future. * (Emotion is the organic source of this mode.) Action comes from emotion.

We should learn what to do in the face of such ignorance. In a dangerous environment ignorance is a special problem. Doing the wrong thing would lead to disaster, if not death. But what happens in a relatively safe environment? A mistake is simply a mistake, and not a dangerous error of judgment. Consequences of action lose their sting.

Action without some kind of notion is panic. Action must be pointed toward some goal, real or imagined. Truth guarantees favorable results. In every case when we act upon the truth, things go as expected. It would be nice, if we could always wait until everything has been proven true or false, but time and circumstances never present themselves so handily. We often act upon unproven data.

Action is basic to the concept of this mode and future. Action upon the proven and certain presents no problem. But what about action based upon assumptions? Action is generally prompted out of commitment to an idea or an ideal. Such commitment is the end of further deliberation. Action then becomes a form of limitation of the thought process, since it is difficult to "think" and "do" at the same time. Action in the assumptive mode of approaching the future is then seen as a cycle, producing that part of the thinking we put aside as foregone conclusions. We need only to observe the difficulty encountered when we try to change the mind or the course of action, of a committed person. First he must be persuaded to stop the ongoing action prompted by his commitment, before he is able to change his course of direction. The totally committed person has stopped thinking or else he uses only a part of his mind which is necessary for him to continue his pursuit.

——— *The term actual future refers to the future we will eventually experience both mentally and physically.

One of the processes prior to commitment is decision. Decision produces anxiety, as it reveals limits. If there were no limits ever placed upon us the decision process would be unnecessary, but because we are limited we must decide where to stop, when to go, what to embrace, what to sacrifice, what to save, what to throw away, etc..

To act upon thought, we have to conclude or condense deliberation to the point where we are motivated to act. Often in the face of poor information we assume things, just to expedite thought or to simplify conclusions. Action in progress is rarely a time of deep meditation. We seek for times and places free of action to begin such deliberations. Action by its nature is not conducive to self conscious thought.

Assumption is a *trick* used to expedite further thought or to begin or maintain action, since we do not want to take the time and resources to consider, ponder, execute a well thought out *judgment*. Assumptive process is a quick incomplete judgment. Assumptions can be a superficial means to allow thought, as when the researcher or scientist assumes certain theories in order to prove them. Otherwise, he might continue waiting for conclusive evidence, which may never come except by trial and error. Because assumptions can be taken as a means to continue thought, assumed "facts" assist us to keep the "ball rolling" as it were, in certain speculative developments. Risk or reward either pressures or lures us to assume, in substitute of certain judgment.

If we accept the saying, "what you don't know won't hurt you" as true, then ignorance is safety. We might justify not waiting for the arrival of the facts by saying "a little assumption is not dangerous." But the proper wait only hurts ignorance. (Waiting principle is investigated further in chapter XI.) The cycle generating the assumptive mode of approaching the future starts from a motive or drive. These motives initiate commitment to some imagined or subconsciously generated condition, event, knowledge or notion. This in turn, prompts action which meets experience. If there are no contradictions to assumption, then further assumptions continue the action. The assumption-think think-assumption cycle used to view the future or the future seen with this cycle is called the Artificial Future. Consenting trust in something or consenting denial of something, makes possible our ability to assume.

The artificial future is influenced by the things that motivate us. If we did not have an artificial future, we could not act except when the truth was known. Because truth is sometimes absent, the artificial future is a substitute for the truth, and it exists until it is revealed as false or just adequate. A well construct artificial future can rival truth however.

The optimist and the pessimist reflect different styles of assumptions in their views of the future. The artificial future of other people is noticed only when it conflicts with our own. Therefore, it may be largely unnoticed and it is often subconscious.

The only one who would not have an artificial future would be God. If God has a perfect foreknowledge, assumptions need not exist in His approach to the future. Without foreknowledge, assumption is necessary to prove reality by experiment.

Our lives are built upon concepts of the future that later may become irrelevant to new conditions. No matter how perfect our dream worlds might be, the hard cold realities often wake us to the actual future, and when it becomes real and present, we are tossed between a rock and a hard place, seeing our assumptions exposed. This constant disillusionment drives the process of belief and trust in the imaginary future to the subconscious level. Our imagined futures, driven underground and dealt with subconsciously produce the mode that generates the artificial future.

CALAMITY REVEALS THE ARTIFICIAL FUTURE

How do we know our artificial future? We need only interview the victims of a drastic life-changing event to find that it exist within us. Earthquakes and hurricanes interrupt what we supposed our future to be. They reveal to us that what we believed to be the itinerary of future events were only vain hopes. If tonight the inside of the earth were to burst like an egg, all our assumptions would be of no consequence. Doomsday talk has been around for ages. It does not alarm any experienced futurist. Yet the point we silhouette against all this is that we live by assumptions so common they are taken for granted. During changes we become able to discern between delusion and illusion, recognizing them for what they are.

The Artificial Future is a constellation of guesses we trust and bank our lives upon. If we have made good guesses then the artificial future will be like the real future. If we have made poor guesses the artificial future will always bring sudden disappointments, if not calamity. With rapid change good guessing is an art worth learning.

Our assumptions are not a logical choice, but they are a subconscious process born of our culture and bred in particular societies. When we visit other countries we are aware of their assumptions because they are strange to us. They conflict with our own. Also, the shock of living in a new culture often opens the mind to the artificial future. Cultural shock or Future shock reveal artificial futures.

IT DOES NOT MATTER IF WE CAN OR CANNOT KNOW

The position of the skeptic or the agnostic is that we can't know anything of the future, because it is beyond our senses and therefore does not exist. This claim takes us to a point where anything that is future is a product of assumption and belief. It is seen as all a guess anyway.

The difference between the artificial future and the imaginary future is this: when we are motivated to act upon the imaginary future it becomes the artificial future. Also the artificial future is largely a product of the subconscious mind and of our emotions, and the imaginary future is of the conscious mind. The deciding factor is the principle of ACTION. The artificial future is actionable imaginations.

Nevertheless skepticism has never built anything, created anything, dared anything, but waits for "someone else" to do it. Before we allow the negative process to operate, we should give creative thoughts dominance. The absolute "knowability" of the future doesn't matter to Futurlogics, because either we know the future, or we must come up with a reasonable substitute. We cannot act without some kind of "future." The question becomes then, "what is the best substitute and how much should we trust this—substitute future?"

WE MUST BE PURPOSEFUL AND ORGANIZED

It seems we can't tolerate lives that have no purpose or direction. Why is this? It seems to be *instinctive*. Maybe our sense of economy places us in a position not to waste the time we have. We live approximately seventy years, and we don't want to do anything that is not fulfilling. Purpose contributes to the quality of our lives. For better or worse act we must and act we do. Organization and quality are direct result if not by products of purpose. The substitute future or artificial future, if well created, will contribute to a better lifestyle. A well constructed Artificial Future can inspire us to find the truth.

PHYSICAL LAW DEMANDS DIRECTION AND PERMANENCE

Time is relative motion compared. It is contrary to the laws of physics that all things move in all directions at once. A body at rest tends to remain at rest and a body in motion tends to remain in motion, until an outside force changes its direction. We are in motion, and it follows from the above law that we have direction, if not purpose.

If we had a perfect foreknowledge, we would be able to move in the temporal environment in complete harmony to all other things in the physical environment. Selecting goals and objectives and having means to fulfill them would be second nature. Our motivational system would have perfect expression. But we are born nearly void of knowledge let alone foreknowledge, and practically powerless to express it.

THE BODY AS A BASIS OF PREDICTION

From birth to death we should be increasing in our knowledge (and foreknowledge). During this time , our body will remain essentially the same. Though one person may be more educated than another, the motivations of people are essentially the same. The fact that we can make a systematic science of psychology is offered as proof. We have the same biological makeup. The main difference between the slow learner and the genius is his intellect. Our motivational system is similar even though the intellect may vary. Our appetites and desires make us able to sympathize, if not empathize with our neighbors' failures and successes. Our motivational system operates with or without knowledge or foreknowledge. No matter how educated we become, we still get hungry and thirsty. Our body acts, interacts and reacts therefore, the body is the foundation of this modal division of the future.

This *substitute future* is created because we are deficient of a real one. The prosthesis here is similar to the production of an artificial limb or organ. It is substituted to expedite "normal" living. We can't just sit around doing nothing because we really don't know what is going to happen next. The prosthetic future we are discussing here performs the same function as the artificial eye, but it suggests more than this, as we shall see as the chapter further develops this modal concept.

We have an either-or situation. Either we know something about the future or we know nothing about it. The philosophy of Futurlogics takes neither position, but says that knowing does not matter because everybody has a "future." True or artificial it makes no difference, since we act and use these futures, either because they are true or because we take them to be true. This makes the investigation of man and prospective thinking continuous and systematic.

Everyone has an artificial future to some degree. We constantly act upon assumptions either consciously or subconsciously. It is a daily event to have these assumptions revealed as such. The old gentleman who said, "the future ain't what it used to be" said it for all of us.

The process of revising the artificial future is a painful one, as seeing the economic future eaten away by inflation and the diminishing prosperity will testify. Revision and updating of the future certainly occur so much so we no longer pay any attention. Portions of the artificial future are sometimes made conscious, but these fringe experiences do not destroy the continuous nature of the future. We find a constant flip-flop between the futures. If we act upon the percept or thought, then we act in the realms of the artificial; if we do not act, but only think about acting, the future remains imaginary. The indecision as to where our percept of the future belongs, is the beginning of conscious understanding of the divisions of the future and of the definition of Futurlogics. Futurlogics is a mode in itself, but it is intended to point us to an eventual encounter with the true future which will be our model.

SUBCONSCIOUS GAMBLING

The calculated risk, the wager, the bet, the dare, the "I'll take a chance" are conscious manifestations of these subconscious workings. As long as we believe we are safe and secure, the artificial future remains below the conscious. If the action prompted by one percept of the artificial future is deemed dangerous or extraordinary, then consciousness of it is brought to the fore.

Every one takes a chances—not just on cards and dice or race horses, but subconsciously. Many times it takes a lifetime to discover we assumed things would happen or had "feelings" which are no longer appropriate. The artificial future is subconscious gambling.

People who wager or bet frequently are bored with life and seek to spice up the commonplace. The gambler gets his excitement from the value of the wager. Events become interesting not for their own sake, but for the "hinge of change" on the turn of events. Those people who are emotionally anesthetized by the commonplace like to tease their artificial future to get more feeling out of the usual, because they lack foreknowledge. Or they are afraid of the commonplace.

UNDERSTANDING THE ARTIFICIAL FUTURE

How do we understand the subconscious? Since the motivations and drives that urge us are mostly unconscious process, this means the artificial future develops below our awareness level. Some might say that we cannot understand it because of its internal nature. But since our actions are the result of these subconscious drives and motivations, understanding comes within the parameters of behavior. Therefore, the artificial future will be best studied from a behaviorally defined system, until the artificial future becomes a reward in itself or a virtue that make waiting pleasant.

One person deals with the future by not thinking of it at all, or so he reports. At first this sounds like escapism, but upon further analysis it is quite appropriate. What he means is he doesn't consciously think of the future. He goes to work, buys a new car on time payments, shops at the grocers for two weeks a time, borrows on future earnings, goes to sleep at night, buys insurance policies, plans a big fishing trip and sets his vacation schedule, phones ahead to make reservations, weeps at funerals, saves money—all this, and he doesn't think of the future! But his behavior says that all he does, has a prospective dimension that extends into the future. We can map his futures by his behaviors.

The conscious logical mind deals easily with the observable, but struggles to deal with intangibles. When we study the future—especially the artificial future—we must suspend conscious logic and be able to turn it off and on as required. **DMP** is part of this ability. Understanding our motivations will be a key to this subconscious future.

We have a hierarchy of drives and motivations. We cannot be hungry and satiated, tired and energetic, sexually attracted and repulsed all at once. There is and order to all our urges and it is rare if not impossible, to have them hit all at the same instant. We have schedules and habits that give these body functions their turns. This may mean that the artificial future may have a schedule and a routine also, that dovetails into the other.

Every organ of the body hues and tenors the behavior and thoughts of man. The brain is an organ containing a force to act also in itself consisting of feelings, sentiments, volition and the higher emotions of love, trust, giving, etc.. These higher motives do not always work in harmony with the appetites of the body, but discordance between them produces the conflicting drives of fatigue or guilt. The artificial future is shaped and generated from this interaction.

We can put off drives, wants and needs for varying lengths of time—some extend beyond the life span. This shapes our individual artificial future(s). The greater our control of the drives that move us to act, the easier it is to see the artificial nature of these "futures." In ancient days, prophets fasted to learn of the future. This may be described in the terminology of this book as subduing the artificial future, in order to make it easier to learn what will truly happen. If we remove the causes of the false future, we can think more clearly and wait for the truth. The value systems of men, indeed their very consciences, spur them to action. The conscience has been traditionally at war with the body's needs. Fasting will allow the artificial future opposed by the conscience, to attenuate. This denial may have been the genesis of the world's religions, since they mainly deal with the future as "afterlife" ignoring personal needs which cause assumptions.

THE ARTIFICIAL FUTURE
MAY APPROXIMATE THE TRUE FUTURE

It may be that someone will generate in the subconscious mind an artificial future that is just as good as the real thing. We are now trying to make artificial hearts that rival the actual heart. This rough comparison shows a possibility that the artificial future may approximate the future so exactly, that it is as good as true. When this happens the artificial future takes on the identity of a *vision*.

If the future is discerned by **DMP,** we can tell the difference between a good imitation and the genuine. Precognition is now under investigation in the laboratories. **DMP** and precognition may be the same thing. While we leave this an undetermined and an open issue, as there are great disputes attached to the possibilities. Whether **DMP** is insight or abstract thought does not matter to the system of Futurlogics, because either opinion should be productive of a clear view of the future(s) of man.

DISCERNING THE MODE

Introspection may reveal some of the artificial future, but such a sustained analysis produces anxiety. Reprocessing of foregone conclusions and 'proven' assumptions is disturbing. To the subconscious everything is true, and it acts accordingly. How much of it is taken for granted and never brought to light? The artificial future persist because men do not like to change. Change produces anxiety also. They ultimately try to arrange everything within, to match the status quo. If you change a man's artificial future, you change the reasons that motivate him. This future is meshed with everything that motivates mankind. It is the deepest rooted.

When there is a collective nature to the artificial future, it makes the revealing of its' nature even more difficult. The culture in which we are raise as children also assumes a future to facilitate the aims of that society. To change the artificial future of that society can bring one into conflict with that society, and there are a host of great men who have met the opposition of bigoted people and not survived. The artificial future handed down from one generation to the next is the hardest to discover from within. In Russia the goals of communism are taught, and sanctions for the visionary who challenges it are strict. The fact that there is an iron curtain evidences the need to confine the Russian population to isolation, because it contributes to the belief in the future of the propagandist, they "foresee." Men always try to make their future match the artificial by engineering it to be so. The synthetic future has this effect when the artificial future is engineered to be "true".

The metaphor is a powerful motivator or motivation often produces a metaphor. When something LIKE another thing is so strongly associated that it is definitive, but really IS not exactly that thing, it is metaphorical.

Metaphors are underestimated in their persuasion of the mind. The Artificial Future and its' mode is driven by such strong associating metaphors. They are emotionally coined tokens of expressions of the future or models. Essentially metaphorical thought produces the Artificial Future by subconscious assumptions.

Study Subjects for the Future-minded in the Artificial Future.

- *Emotional Attachment to "Visions", Theories, Guesses . . . .*
- *False Peer Reviews or No Peer Reviews.*
- *Disregarding Insight and Intuition.*
- *Proper Social Relationships vs. Clinical Approach.*
- *Recognizing Hidden Value or Gold Mining Data.*
- *Explaining Concepts in Simplicity is the Best Answer.*
- *Premature Judgment vs. Waiting too Long.*

Chapter VIII

SYNTHETIC FUTURE

THE CREATIVE MODE AND THE SYNTHETIC FUTURE

The key to the creative mode is the hand. The hand is the mind's extension. With it we can manipulate things around us. Civilization is made possible through the things man has made. In the arts the mind and the hand become as one. The hand enables us to express and change our lot. The capabilities possessed in conjunction with the intelligence we develop, give us power to change even our future. All our plans and preparations, goals and purposes, all our visions of tomorrow could come true by our hands. [Hand(s) is the organic source of this mode.]

How does this mode compare with the previously described modes? Notice how in the theater the play is created. The drama brings insights into the first two modes, and also into the third mode, the creative mode. There are at least three elements basic to the stage presentation: the director/producer, the actors, and the audience. Given the script, the actors perform the drama and the audience sees the final production. The best plays are those in which the audience becomes totally involved and forgets they are at the theater. The actors often lose themselves in their roles and lure the audience to suspend their disbelief in favor of the total involvement. The director/producer functions to bring it all together—the lights, the costumes, music, publicity, and other aspects.

The synthetic future as a product of the creative mode is similar to the function of the director/producer of the play. The analogy suggests that the future can be a product of our endeavor. The world is seen as a theater metaphorically in which we can stage our play; however, we can be more than the players.

Folklore substantiates this modal approach to the future. The old sayings, "the future is made, not waited for," "opportunity knocks but once," "plan ahead and avoid waste and mistakes," "a stitch in time save nine," and others encourage us in our power over our course in life. We need not be passive observers of the future, or mindless robots to the will of our circumstances, or of the single unchangeable "to be." We can change our lot and because of this, we may look at the future as a resource rather than a role in a play. We can write our own script. We can realize our dream(s), imagination(s), our artificial future(s).

The future seen through this present *creative mode* is all that man will produce either by his action or his thoughts, it is our synthetic future. From the time man was conscious of himself, he sought to change things for more desirable conditions—and not for mere survival but to overcome and to succeed.

As our ancestors learned to control their environment and to prepare themselves against the uncontrollable, they made changes we now take for granted. They built cities, life-styles, philosophies. The synthetic future is therefore all things man will yet bring into existence. Anything "observed to occur less man" is then the natural future. In the creative mode the natural future and the absolute future, are viewed as resources to be drawn upon, to be built upon. They become a *basis* for our guiding designs. All the desires and wishes of our hearts work towards the synthetic future. However, we have a greater impact upon the future than we know. Our very presence upon the Earth and not just our acts as man, influences the future. The definition of this future might be more precisely described as, the impact made upon nature by man's presence and designs. Obviously if there were no persons on the Earth there would be no possible synthetic future, only the natural future or natural base will exist. But this is like the philosophical question, if a tree fell where no one was to hear it would there be a sound?

Life has been balancing itself to a harmony of extraordinary complexity for eons of time. From virus to elephant, from diatoms to whales, all have settled into a symphony of give and take. We are learning now the results of the old saying that, "a little knowledge is dangerous." For the things we have manufactured in the developmental stages of our learning are now, upsetting the intricate balances nature has built up to a stable min-max (A term which means that minimum condition(s) trigger a change and maximum condition(s) trigger a counter-change) life-sustaining system. Only long-range prediction of the impact of the creative mode upon the future, can settle the effect of any newly applied technological function upon the environment. We must study the synthetic future, to see the impact of man on the ecology of the planet's life support system, and its limits to repair itself.

Man's impact upon nature began long before we were aware of the ramifications of our acts and creations. It was felt generally that nature would take care of any mistakes we made. Indeed the corrosive forces of nature were so great, that it was a matter of constant upkeep and maintenance to keep anything from reducing to its organic source and material. But now we produce synthetic non biodegradable materials to such a perfected state, the opposite problem of indestructible waste exists. We make synthetic rubber, plastic, oil, leather, wood, etc. We are even trying to make synthetic man, as we see from the latest advancements of the medical field. Could man's inventions overwhelm the systems in nature?

This approach to the future becomes a mode when, what man does is emphasized to the point that nature is secondary or forgotten. For example, the city dweller who says that milk comes from the supermarket, disallowing the purpose of the cow in milk production, has lost sight of milk's connection with nature. During the exercise of our powers to change, we create a modal bubble that is burst when nature goes on a rampage. Given a long-term drought, we soon rediscover our interdependence if not dependence upon nature.

BENEFITS OF CONTROL

We have raised ourselves above the animals in that we no longer depend upon what we forage, scavenge or hunt. By farming animals and raising crops, we have set ourselves free to expand our civilization, by the cultivation of the materials we need to survive to raise our level of living. The maximum number of people that can be sustained on this planet with a given standard of living, with a given technology to produce the necessities of quality living, is a figure that changes with each technique of producing our needs synthetically. The so called sustainable levels can be altered by improved technology. Sometimes, if we outstrip our science, we begin to talk of overpopulation. We then, through necessity learn new methods that will make life easier at an even higher standard of living, then it will be easier to accept the natural growth of the population. This is proportional to our knowledge of farming the Earth and using its resources positively, instead of squandering it and ourselves on war, where only a very few benefit from this waste. This vista is a result of looking at the future through the prism of the *creative mode*. The ability to adapt has given us great freedom and power, to maintain a high level of success. One may be drawn to conclude that this is the best mode to approach the future. Perhaps it is, with proper respect to prudent creativity.

But along with the power to allow more populated levels of civilization, comes an even greater power to destroy it all. If we exercise the negative side of our power to change the face of the earth, it is possible that the synthetic future on this planet will be in the form of our own charred remains when viewed through the creative mode. Then the *natural future* will be the sterile remnants of our used-up elements. *Proper control* should be exercised, if the synthetic mode is used in dealing with the future or predicting it. Control can come from anarchy or tyranny, from socialism or individual responsibility, from a sovereign king or a constitutional republic, from spiritual evil or spiritual righteousness, from radical ideologies or common sense. We choose.

We see today the conflict of the natural future and the synthetic future. Protect man by using the raw materials of the earth, or protect the environment at the expense of man. We might question, "who shall control this mode and how shall it be implemented?" Some may arrogate themselves to be guardians of the Earth and its biosphere but what is their true motive? Is environmentalism sincere, or is it a ploy to control for controls sake? But can we overcome our lack of control with common sense? With these questions in mind, we see that the synthetic future and its mode has drawbacks also. It becomes very true that the meek will inherit the Earth, but only when the meek are those who do not trust brute force as the only solution. A wise harmonious cooperation with the natural forces could be the best way to an economical use of resources. The age of sensible use of energy is here, and the meek are those who will not govern others by force, but the teachers of freedom will inherit the earth.

The key to comprehending the synthetic future is to know the person(s) who will produce it. Again the unit of measure here is man himself, as it is in everything. What man does, and is, causes the synthetic future. "Know thyself, and to thine own self be true." The first frontier that one should explore is in one's self. We should apply creativity inwardly even to ourselves. It is possible to transform. Our understanding of ourselves must be balanced, for we have a tendency to evaluate ourselves in terms of our technological capabilities. Let us consider a problem: If all the underdeveloped countries on Earth were to be industrialized to the extent of the United States, the consumption of raw materials would be multiplied many times the possible output of the available materials. (The U.S. uses per capita more than all the other countries combined.) Technology is not enough. We should learn how and when to apply the technology, and acknowledge the related side effects in non-laboratory conditions, but in free environmental test, to get the true results. We must not be victims of false science.

THE SOURCE OF OUR GOALS

What is the source of the goals, plans and objectives that guide our activities to produce the synthetic mode/future? When cities are planned and laws enacted to change the existing status quo. From whence do these plans come? From whom do these purposes originate? Who predicted the results of these actions? The purpose of Futurlogics is to find the source of the ideals, goals, futures, directing forces, and "visions" that enable our leaders to shape our lives, by shaping our "futures." The Purpose of studying modes and the psychology behind them is to bring to understanding the creation of the mapped futures, we never seem to question these maps, but accept their influence in our lives. Democracy, that is, a free democracy demands each citizen participates in shaping his country's future. A republic prevents a democracy from being self destructive. This is brought home when we begin to think about the emerging science of social engineering, and the creation of the synthetic man.

Not being aware of the side effects of our industrialization and synthetic input into the environment, we learn too late that what we once considered harmless has accumulated to danger levels. Non-biodegradable and excessive waste concentration in small areas present problems that were not foreseen. In highly populated cities like New York, garbage disposal is a major problem. A few decades ago it was ignored. The synthetic future becomes a mode when we do not acknowledge side effects. Some say that side effects are only a matter of perspective and some times the side effects are the goal. We should be then aware of such social engineering, when the side effects are the actual goals.

War—the conflict between two sets of synthetic futures—brings out the last point at which the synthetic future becomes a mode, and that is, we do not always create things for the benefit of our fellows. We design machines and weapons to destroy. War breaks down both natural and synthetic environments. War is not reality, it is anti-reality. Therefore, if the synthetic mode is destructive, we lose touch with the actual future. Modes that do not lead us to a better understanding of reality are substitutes used in place of truth. Wars come from our inability to produce all that we need or from greed, therefore they are a breakdown in the synthetic future.

How much of who and what we are, has come from the hidden forces of those who try to shape us into the kinds of people useful to their designs? What will happen to their followers, if they become no longer useful? What restraints are employed to control those who wish to engineer us and our society to hidden designs? What portion of our personality is synthetic and what part is a natural product of our own free choice? To shape the future of a person is to control his motivations, and thereby control the things by which he guides his life. The system of Futurlogics will reveal the manipulations of unscrupulous persons, who will exercise the power to change the seat of our motivational systems, which are the "futures of the mind." When we are made conscious of where we obtained our notions of the future, then we will better plan, decide, prepare, predict, wait, motivate, choose, in short, to do anything that is prospective and oriented toward the future. We ensure being a free people rather than an enslaved democracy, by being more knowledgeable of everything, including the future that shapes our motivations and goals. Participation in the future is not an option.

COMMITMENT

The volitive restrictions found in the absolute mode take another direction in the synthetic mode. Here we find another technique that avoids this conflict by rewarding it to submission, even with minimal personal effort. The objective that produces this future places us in the strange position of *sacrificing our will to gain our will*. We commit ourselves to the operations of a plan to create a future that the synthetic mode will generate. In other words, we voluntarily limit the range of volition by saying that we are concentrating our efforts and thoughts to the accomplishment of the design. Commitment is the point where we assign our activities to the plan, that will make the achievement of our goals and objective real. A dynamic between safety and freedom.

Civilization is a commitment. When we look to the future with the synthetic mode, we will be confronted with a commitment. The persons who works under this mode will be captured by the mode itself. City dwellers will be more subject to the demands of civilization, than the rural farmer who is practically independent, producing to meet most of his own needs. Sometimes civilization can threaten self-sufficiency.

LOOKING AT THE FUTURE
THROUGH THE CREATIVE MODE

We should realize now there will always be things and events that we can never create. There are limits. The ultimate limit may be man himself. God who seems to leave us to ourselves may one day reveal those limits. How much energy and power would it require to accomplish all the dreams of the mind? If we learn to work with nature, it may not require any energy at all, except that of intelligence. Making nature work for us is the art of creating a synthetic future, we can live in. Brute force and exercising muscles in every direction with no control or forethought, will produce a synthetic future, that no one should tolerate.

Creativity separates man and animals. It is a great gift but as with genius, it can be misused. We must learn to farm the deserts and the oceans, and moderate the weather. We must create a means of living peacefully, and with freedom for all the Earth's citizens. The planet becomes smaller as we gain more power to change it, and as we make devices to overcome the forces of nature.

But energy is central to creativity. We need energy, mental and physical, to create. Follow the money yes, but seek the source of all energy and power. The planetary society will be ushered in with forecasts of doom, if we continue to cheapen human life and rights. The potential however is Utopian in scope.

The variety of our physical environment is almost beyond comprehension. Nature has both order and variety. As we learn more about our Earth, we gain a better perspective of the synthetic mode and Mother Nature working out her own problems. Her surprises are evidence of how dependent we are upon her.

Yet her surprises are really no surprise, for we have seen them before. We expect most of what occurs, even though precise prediction still eludes us. Perfection of these skills necessary to prognostication of time, date and place are till in the offing. Earthquakes, floods, eruptions of volcanoes, solar spots, hurricanes and such are all still in the infant stage of prediction. Shark tooth replacement, bird migration, etc., are familiar to us. Though we know these expressions of her moods, we have yet to see what she has in store for us, if we tamper with intricate balances. It could be that such holocaust awaits in the wings that fear and trembling are in good taste when we approach her secret parts.

All that Mother Nature has done can only be guessed at. Her mistakes are extinct and buried. The present balance is the result of all the trial and error of the past and long waits for renewal. The race of man is a latecomer, and we have not learned all the mistakes possible. With the threat of an unbalance ecology, the study of the natural future has been emphasized. We have been forced to eat some of our worst mistakes. A better understanding of the natural future will give us a good chance to survive on this space-island Earth.

We enact laws to limit our input into the natural order of things. If we were eliminated from the planet, then everything would reduce to a continuous state of naturally occurring events. This is the extreme vision of the "environmentalist" who wishes to preserve samples of nature for surviving grandchildren. But we will have to provide for our children the best we can, taking from the environment only the things we need to survive and progress. The balance between these divided interests are discussed with strained relationships. The contest between the preservation of the natural order and the satisfaction of needs, is going to meet new intensity in the future. Our laws are only as good as our ability to control ourselves with the others we share this Earth. Our indiscriminate use of technology requires that we take a second look. Balancing restraints will be a constant point of attention in the developing synthetic future.

LONG RANGE VIEW

The long range effects of things, we were either unaware of or unconcerned about, are straining our ecological limits. Elk, buffalo, and bear abounded in the grasslands of Kentucky. Today all the buffalo in Kentucky are in the zoo. The life support zone on our earth is so critical that most of its operations are studied to prevent the ecology, from being upset to such an unrecoverable state, that we may forever alter the normal traits of Mother Nature. We do not want new normals for her.

It might be argued that man himself is a natural thing, and as such could be lumped into the whole concept of the natural future. If this is the case, then the natural future takes upon it the similitude of the synthetic future. Some of the distinctions of the natural future become diffused in the merge. However, these divisions are for the sake of making the study of the future easier and more manageable. When we have studied all the pieces separately, we shall "sum them up", and we will find that the whole is greater than the sum of its parts—a synergy. Then deceit will vanish.

Life throws many variables into the computation which strain the reaches of the physics and related fields. Once the element of life is introduced, new complexities of infinite scope are impacted on the relatively simple physical sciences. Bioscience must introduce us gradually to ourselves. The absolute future, natural future(s), and the synthetic future(s) can only exist simplistically, when the variables of the introspections of man are subdued. The natural future becomes apparent when we eliminate man or the self-consciousness of man. Introspection is the basis of the next mode the prospective mode.

Study Subjects for the Future-minded in the Synthetic Future.

● *Valuing, Honoring, Creativity and Genius.*
● *Foremost Authorities in Research and their Value in Planning.*
● *Recognizing How Revolutionary Ideas Form or Transform.*
● *Respecting the Non Experts Perspective in Futuring the Future.*
● *Deep Research and Casual Study.*
● *Benefits of Research to Extend Life and Improve Health.*
● *Respecting Power of Natural Forces Benefits Future-mindedness.*

Chapter IX

PARADIGM FUTURE

THE PARADIGM FUTURE AND THE MODEL MODE

Knowledge of the future seems to be instinctive. "None of us" are completely void of any knowledge of the future. We may not know details but the general notion of its existence is well accepted. "All of us" have a degree of prescience. Even if this prescience is vague and general, it points our mind to look forward or inward in a metaphoric way. From this vague knowledge we can shape and see the future as if it were a mode–prospective mode–if you will. The future we see through our "instinctive" knowledge is the paradigm future. The paradigm future is our estimation of the future from the non-specific form of intuition. It is also the sense of the future we have gained through using the other modes in synthesis. The first five modes can generate this mode. (Conscious-knowledge is the organic source of this mode.)

The historical mode, the observational mode, the imaginary mode, the assumptive mode, and the creative mode all give us a certain degree of prescience, enabling us to relate to the future. The accumulation of data gained through these modes gives us a sense that we can use to determine future events. Thinking about knowledge gained from the other modes to determine even more, generates the prospective cycle and the prospective mode to use the paradigm future.

MODEL AND/OR MODAL

The prospective approach to the future is both a mode and a model. In the divided futures, we have analyzed, it stands as very important. It is a mode because we use partial knowledge to obtain further knowledge of the future. It is a model because the success of achieving some knowledge of the future gives us an ideal or model, to pattern further approaches. Because this mode is at the same time also a model, it is central to Futurlogics.

The prospective cycle can be seen or used as a mode also, if we realize that most persons generally divide the future into "short range" and "long range." If we use only short-range future facts to determine long-range future events and conditions, then the modal properties of distortion are possible. Also, if we take the long-range facts to determine short-range events and conditions, then the modal characteristics are again evident. In order to prevent our knowledge of the future from becoming a mode, we have to let the future naturally piece itself together. Likening the future to ourselves is modal. Adapting ourselves to the future is archetypal/model. Being over-zealous with a little knowledge, and attempting to squeeze this knowledge into a comprehensive foreknowledge in the beginning, changes the model properties of the prospective cycle to modal limitations. When this prospective approach to the future is model, it is synergistic, and the whole is greater than the sum of its parts or the other modes.

If we have a good knowledge of the future—nearly a foreknowledge in definition and specification of dates and events—then the modal effect is minimized and the model aspect is maximized. In simpler words, the more we know of the future, the more we can know. Conversely, the less we know, the less we can know. Ignorance breeds confusion. Success is the best basis for more success.

THE SUBCONSCIOUS AND THE PROSPECTIVE MODE

To a Californian New York is real, but it cannot be directly experienced. If he doubts that New York exists, he needs only visit the state and see for himself its actuality. For the most part we accept the maps and reports of those who have been there. Likewise we have learned to prove parts of the future we know by waiting for some aspect of it, to test its actuality. After a few such tests, we find it is expensive and unnecessary to test all the things we know of the future, so we accept them as we would a map of New York state.

The whole map of the earth is accepted by random sample test of some part of the earth, to see if it is in compliance with the map. It is not necessary or impossible to go to every part of the planet to see if the entire map is correct. After we gain a confidence level, we are assured the entire map is true. The prospective mode of approaching the future is also this kind of confidence build-up.

The confidence tests we use will give us the trust we need to learn of the future from the known parts of the future, which is modeling the future. We say that the sun will rise tomorrow. We learn to accept this without question. Prolonged thought to prove that the sun will rise can cause doubt, and even a flash of fear. We learn to laugh at such fears and say everybody "knows" the sun will rise tomorrow. This is seen as unnecessary worry and it is not practical.

Because of this most of what we know of the future remains at the subliminal level, which is nearly at the subconscious level of thought. Simply the usual logic we use to prove things generally does not work, and always causes trouble and anxiety when we deal with the future. Dealing with present realities, we find these techniques work fine and tend to give us a sense of certainty. However only our subconscious mind can handle the seeming "surreality" of futurity. If the future seems like a dream, it is because it maybe or it may *be*.

Things learned through the prospective cycles are self-evident and intuitively obvious, and may only be proved by further prospective thought. They should be seen by a non-objective method. Again, this is where the model of Futurlogics and **DMP** can be seen in the prospective approach to the future. Remember **DMP** represents both insight and intuition at the same time—model/modal.

We know that eventually the sun will burn out and the earth will freeze' that is, if the sun follow it's expected course. But to use this knowledge as a basis of action is not practical because of the billions of years between now and that event. By that time man will have found another planet and/or sun to take its place. If our knowledge of the future directly applies to the present and we can relate to it, it is a model. If however, we try to work out everyday-problems and events from a remote future, the modal effect is present. Foreknowledge should put us into harmony with reality, not cause discordance. The Bible states, "take no thought for the morrow . . . the morrow will take thought for itself." We should not concern ourselves with things beyond that which we can relate to, unless the object is pure research of the future. The saying that "a little knowledge is dangerous" is true here. Vague notions of the future, even though true, are sometimes worse than no knowledge at all, if we over react to them.

The amount or quality of the knowledge of the future decides whether it is mode or model. If the foreknowledge is extensive and action sure and positive, then the paradigm future is a harmonious model. But without meaningful behavior the prospective cycle is a mode. Finally, when Futurlogics is learned, the paradigm future becomes a model. The future should be understandable to be practical. All foreknowledge begins as subconscious prescience. Indeed by definition foreknowledge is conscious knowledge of the future, and prescience is the subliminal/subconscious inklings of foreknowledge. In the Paradigm Future, if we use foreknowledge to further study the future it is a model approach, or if the vague subconscious prescience is used as a source, it becomes a mode of approach. Both approaches come from the prospective cycle.

Next is a note that was not in the original printing of 1983 but may help in developing principles to think in the prospective dimensions:

The tools to think can be turned into themselves and applied to thinking about thinking itself. This is metacognition or (thinking about thinking.) When a metaphor is developed, it is using existing thinking or knowledge to describe the yet unknown. We can use accepted "known" to describe the notional or the intuitive hunch. A seed of the future is the notional or hunch level of our cognizance of the future. When the developing information from the seeds of the future produce an expanding spiral of thought or in other words produce a vista, it is a model. When the developing information from the seeds of the future, produce a focusing and refining specification of the future, where the refined information is action enabled, it is modal. If you are to look at the future in broad terms the first method that produces a model is the best method. If you are to look at the future in time and space with objectives or goals to fill agendas, it is modal prediction. When the broad picture is seen then deduction can refine and define to the specificity needed, for preparation and scheduling using this deductive reasoning. When patches of the future are achieved, then these collections of perspectives can be reasoned with, by inductive techniques to suppose the greater overall vision or vista of the future. Which of these techniques is of greater accuracy is a matter of application and intuition. These methodologies should assist each other, under the **DMP** holistic fashion or approach. Use both to look ahead according to the dovetail of appropriateness.

What are the seeds of the future? **DMP** enables the acquisition of the seeds and seeds sprout to greater views or intuitions. The metaphor of seed is used to imply all the growth potential of new knowledge begetting new knowledge.

COMMENT: Metacognition studies is like future studies, in that there is a capacity to handle abstract thought required for both studies. Futurlogics, which is a study of prospective thinking, then is a specific application of metacognition applied to dealing with the future and/or the concept of the future. The metaphoric thinking systems are devices to stimulate more thought about thought. Since it is easier to handle the metaphors that the pure abstraction of the direct thoughts on thoughts, there is a degree of concreteness to the thoughts. However as holistic thought or **DMP** is developed then metacognition need not be so difficult, but is a form of meditation.

SUMMARY AND FUTURLOGICS

Perhaps other ideas can be made into divisions of the future, and then into modes; but what we have studied will be of general application and can serve in a broad discussion of the future and how we deal with our beliefs concerning it.

To briefly summarize the divisions and the modes, we make some concise definitions for purposes of reference:

- **Absolute future** is a future described in the parameters of the retrospective thought and linear extension of the past;
- **Natural future** is the future described in the parameters of sensory observation where personal objectivity is strictly observed;
- **Imaginary future** is all that man imagines the future to be;
- **Artificial future** is the internal future generated by the subconscious levels of thought spawned by the forces which cause us to act;
- **Synthetic future** is described in terms of the mind's extension, the hand—it is the act of creativity;
- **Paradigm future** is the foreknowledge we have which lacks definition and detail, but which shapes our view of the future. It is precognition. It becomes both a mode and a model.

The above divisions become symbols and terms of the parametric descriptions of the future that we have referred to as modes. They are metaphors. Modes are the results of cycles—or closed circuit thinking—as in the see-know, in the see-believe. Very often when we are exposed to new things we interpret them by language with which we are familiar, and we are often misled because of the mechanics of the familiar terms.

Futurlogics is the balanced use of all the modes which neutralizes the modal distractions as we envision the future. It becomes the **DMP** contact to the study of the future. It points to truth, which is knowledge of the three phases of the temporal environments—past, present, and future. Futurlogics is the perfected mode of minimize distortion from familiar terms use to describe the future.

None of us have a perfect knowledge of how we conceive the future, nor do we have complete foreknowledge. But the "future(s)" we do understand can be improved. **DMP** is the only "contact" we have with the ulterior realities we call futurity. **DMP** has been left purposely ambiguous, because the exact nature of this "contact" is not clear until we perfect the system of Futurlogics. Futurlogics will set up such an attitude of mind that full contact with the future through **DMP** can be achieved. This is personal and cannot be learned through group-think.

Five stages of growth can be recognized in our orientation to the future. First, *innocence*; second, *proxy future*, or "any future is better than no future;" third, Futurlogics or *prototype future*; fourth, *prescience*; fifth **DMP** direct mental contact. The sixth stage is foreknowledge.

The essential point to this is that we don't have a perfect knowledge of the future, or a perfect foreknowledge. So we come up with a proxy future, subject to revision when we discover its limitations. How we revise it is the thrust of this book. Futurlogics is the systematic revision of these proxy futures toward a prototype that will point to the truth, which becomes the final objective—*foreknowledge*!

Traffic signs indicate road conditions and maps guide us through unknown territories. So we should use Futurlogics as a guide to direct us toward our objective. Futurlogics is not the future—it is a means, a guidepost, a map, to help us on our way.

We should always be conscious of how the parameters(modes) of thinking about the future lead us away, from **DMP** contact with future realities. **DMP** is our most intimate contact with the future, and to allow any distraction will result in a distorted view of things to come.

The minimum requirement of Futurlogics is to be able to use more than one mode. This is where conscious "paradigm shifting" in either direction is a tool to probe the future. This free-floating effect of transferring awareness to the mode in which one is operating, is necessary to see ahead clearly. Discerning the origin of any idea, notion, or feeling is the key to accurate prediction. Tracing each idea to the mode in which we are thinking will develop this ability. **DMP** will be the final result. Remember to use only one mode is to have others think for you. **DMP** is truly thinking for oneself.

RELATION TO THE ACADEMIC WORLD

In the world we live, we are surrounded by academic disciplines. All the sciences set forth points and areas concerning the future but they are specialized. If we have been able to detach ourselves from the narrowness of the views that any specific approach to the future might produce, the special patterns of thought to which Futurlogics ascribes, enables us to look objectively at these various allusions. Any futurist must be able to detach himself from the present and see from another point in space/time. This detached, free-floating perspective is necessary to probe the future, and it is the outcome of Futurlogics. If a futurist cannot free himself from his method of obtaining data, the procedures and logics of the methods will inject themselves into the resulting scenario of the future. To see a "paradigm shift" one must be able to get to a *third perspective* to view the two paradigms shifting back and forth or *toggling*.

In order to look at the future from the standpoint of a generalist rather than that of a specialist, an overall attitude must be acquired so all the predictions of the specialized fields of research can fit into the larger scheme of things. In the academic role, the futurist will eventually come in at the end of all the other studies. Since the future is a result of all kinds of causes, the futurist should have the most expansive view of all the disciplines in education. Unbalanced input from the academic system of today from a dominant discipline is tantamount to the modal effect that we have been discussing in the distorting effect of the six modes. The psychology and mentality of today's futurist will eventually arrive at the implied meaning of **DMP**, as it has been outlined due to the organic origins of the cycles and the mode produced from them.

Another side note is that each person's personality will necessitate that **DMP** be the result of intuitive discovery. This has been the thrust of this study and must remain so, as long as the techniques and teaching methods of futurism are in their beginning stages, before a structured teaching system for studying the futurist psychology can develop.

DMP is an intuitive discovery. It cannot be taught, nor can we know the exact nature of **D**IRECT **M**IND **P**ERCEPTION—*insight* or **D**IRECT **M**ENTAL **P**ROCESS—*intuition*. However, these process or perceptions are a natural and inherent part of thinking. We use them all the time, but we are rarely in conscious control of them. Futurlogics offers a way to tap and use the natural abilities of the mind to derive information from the future and our conceptions of it.

Although **DMP** cannot be taught, Futurlogics can, and Futurlogics leads to the discovery of **DMP**. Futurlogics enables us to alternate from one mode to another freely, so that we can approach the future from many perspectives even many paradigms, and evade the distortion of a narrow approach. Even though the beginnings are mechanical, when the process is internalized, we should find the emergence of **DMP**. How do we internalize the procedure of Futurlogics? It is by practice and conscious effort, and it will eventually become habit and unconscious procedure. It is during these beginning stages the sense of **DMP** should be felt and be discernible in the thought process.

We must try the different modes and be able to use them all. Also, we must wean ourselves from excessive favoritism of one mode. Resistance upon leaving a favorite mode is the biggest obstacle to **DMP** we will encounter, many an enterprise has failed because they failed to adapt to a "paradigm shift." But it is essential that our thoughts be clear, candid, and impersonal. The future is everything new, and not yet colored by prejudicial bias. We must be childlike to look toward the future effectively.

It is best to study the modes and the thought processes that precipitate their use and adherence, in thinking about the future (or any other subject of an abstract nature for that matter). Thorough understanding of the ways people think about the future, can help us avoid the pitfalls inherent in undertaking the prediction of the future. Sometimes it is just as useful to understand why we have failed, as to succeed and not understand why.

Futurlogics helps us understand our failures and points us to success. **DMP** contact with the future is the most positive experience we can have, because it liberates the mind to think as it was meant.

Being able to use the different modes, we can become able to recognize the origin of each idea. When we can trace each idea, concerning the future, then any idea that is a product of **DMP** is recognizable. **DMP** is itself a discerning ability, to trace to the source or the origin of ideas.

Again, when we first try to investigate the future it is as though we are looking through a kaleidoscope—every time we move, it changes. But if dissembled it is exquisitely simple: a few pieces of colored glass, a diffusing medium to destroy fine detail and enhance general form, and a tube to direct the line of vision to the mirrors . . . **DMP** then, is understanding this kaleidoscope of our mind seeing the future.

SUMMARY UPDATE

THE PARADIGM OF FUTURLOGICS © 2010

Futurlogics is a "study it out in your mind" technique. It is pre-knowledge. Pre-knowledge is unconcluded thinking that will prepare the mind to see the thing(s), that otherwise would be "overlooked." It shows that prior knowledge will influence markedly, succeeding learning or knowledge.

Building a vision for the future with its attending goals and vistas, is best approached through the view, that the future must be seen through six thought streams, or modes, and further synergized with holistic thinking to a pattern/model.

The benefit of studying a thinking system such as Futurlogics may be illustrated with the following example:

With the advent and advancement of the computer and other modern inventions, there is now time to do what man does better than the machines, which is really think and make good decisions. The human brain is so flexible, that it can have millions of thinking systems for every purpose. Man must really learn to think again. Perhaps children think the way we should, and we need a reminder to get back to that natural thought process. Computers and computer modeling have given man time to think, therefore the winner in the competition to come will be, the one who is thinking best! Top management will be equal in software and data processing as the software companies unify, so the differences will be seen in the companies who can "out think" their market competitors. Computers process data. People process knowledge. Foreknowledge is leverage to change the future and secure success.

Next is a sample of a Futurlogics' organically defined prospective thinking session. Futurlogics is predominantly a private thinking system, but can be used in a group setting. ("group thinking" is useful in some conditions, but "private thinking" is useful in all conditions.) "private thinking" is organic and "group thinking" is externally defined thinking. "Group thinking" is artificially defined.

Remember:

• A **cycle** is a thought routine.
• A **mode** is a deductive thought routine.
• A **model** is an inductive thought routine.

First start by reviewing known historical facts, legends, writings on the subject of the session, realizing of course, that the past is not history. This may establish the motives for the research. Now in this review, point out any repetition that will forecast the future.
(A history of the past gives meaning and tradition. Futurlogics retrospective cycle generates the retrospective mode, which produces the absolute future or solution. This cycle is very defensive of "obsolete ideas" and has the effect of volitional restriction, which blunts the creative edge. These expressions are usually so called "proven ideas.")
Second take the scientific method, and look at the project of the session with a clinical approach. This is similar to some facets of scanning the current information, and gathering it with no prejudgment.
(Observation gives us sequential order, clarity, definition and quantification. Futurlogics observational cycle generates the observational mode, which produces the natural future or solution. This is where we step back "be still," and look at the propositions with the neutral form of learning. These are ideas every body can see or are in consensus. This is similar to the scientific approach to discovery. This is in part a "left brain" approach.)
Third employ the imagination by projecting ideas to the future using extended associations. This maybe a definition of "to consider." The word consider comes from the Latin "com" meaning with and "sidus," "sideris" meaning star or stars. Thus consider defined from its roots in Latin, would be rendered "with the stars."

Matthew 6:28-29 28 And why take ye thought for raiment? Consider the lilies of the field, how they grow; they toil not, neither do they spin: 29 And yet I say unto you, That even Solomon in all his glory was not arrayed like one of these.

(What if those lilies "stars" of the field "heaven" were metaphors? Imagination gives us possibilities and brainstorms. Futurlogics imaginary cycle generates the imaginary mode, which produces the imaginary future or solution. These are positive extensions or extrapolations and unusual associations. Thought production that generate ideas for the sake of ideas is the aim.)

Fourth conduct a "What IF" session next and extend logically. This is the effect/affect of substitutions, to roll thought on to greater deliberation. This is essentially the process/perceptive technique of "VISIONING." This maybe defined as "to ponder" or to weigh things out or to think with the heart. The word ponder comes from the Latin words "ponderare, pondus, ponderis" meaning "to weigh."

(Assumptions/faith gives us movement "food for thought," and continuity in the face of the unknown, in other words at the frontiers. Futurlogics assumptive cycle generates the assumptive mode, which produces the artificial future or solution. These are "what if" extensions or extrapolations and imaginative associations. This is where experiments and risks are suspended, to see what probably will happen. Proofs can be generated by assuming certain things are true, for the sake of continuing the research. This is essentially a "dry lab" of the creative mode. Here is where hypothesizing takes place. In other terms, this is the first creation or a spiritual creation, if you will.)

Fifth see what you can make happen or deliberately create now, by providing a conducive environment to free thought with a constructive nature. By this time we have considered, pondered, and are now creating. This is "fission and fusion" of ideas to get new ideas. This may require deep meditation.

(Planning and preparation are leverages for making or designing the future. Futurlogics creative cycle generates the creative mode, which produces the synthetic future or solution. This is synthesis not analysis! Here is where ideas are reified. In other terms this is the second creation, a bringing to temporal reality the plans and hopes of the future. This is in part a "right brain" approach.)

Sixth, where is IT all going? Now envision the probable direction the discussion and discoveries will take this session. This mental technique is founded upon all five of the previous modes/models just outlined.

(Prospective thinking uses 'where is it all going?' type to go further. Futurlogics prospective cycle generates the prospective mode, which produces the paradigm future or solution. This is nurturing of the abstract ideas to see ahead. This is re-visioning . This is where the ideas are projected further up the timeline. A strong vision will be of great use in the "six modes.")

Author Thomas S. Kuhn, who has given us the concept of the "paradigm shift," proposed, that the catalyst to revolutionary change in science is the paradigm. This is discussed in his seminal paper "The Structure of Scientific Revolution." In this paper, the very posit of science is under investigation which simply stated is, that objective observed facts will cause knowledge to grow evenly, without subjective input being injected into the research. Yet, no matter how science is defined, such progress in scientific knowledge is and was not smoothly discovered, but scientific knowledge came in fits and starts, bits and bursts. Subjective influences do exist in science, and they are the result of the "paradigm."

This has been a controversial topic, but simplistically it can be stated thusly, "the brain behind the 'senses' make sense of the 'senses' input." Subjectivity can not be eliminated. The brain is the center of science, and can not be ignored to produce the desired objectivity. Science should "calibrate the brain" to see objectively, as it does with all it's other instruments. At the center of the brain is it's own chemistry, it's own electrical energy and it's own pre-knowledge, which is the method of learning and **DMP.**

If any of this is ignored, science is not complete in it's study. Therefore subjectivity and objectivity need balance, and should not work at odds, but must work together. Science that does not recognize the influence of the spirit, or the mind, is not true science.

The paradigm mode should reveal a "paradigm shift." That is, if we have applied the five previous modes appropriately. We should perceive change, at least in the subjective view of the data, the facts, the information, the knowledge itself. If you have not detected any transforming newness, which feels creative or is at least innovative, then repeat the cycle/modes streaming from the beginning, until there is detected at least a mild "paradigm shift."

It really does not matter, which of the future(s) have a definite shift, important here is the mental force to obsolete "old knowledge," by replacing it with "new knowledge." After one detects the "paradigm shift," then the Paradigm Mode becomes the Paradigm Model. There should be a revolution in knowledge to follow. This may be defined as the "paradigm lift."

At this stage of the Futurlogics session, as many as six futures are generated from the cycles and modes of futurlogics, as we examine the futures to see the impact, the newly generated ideas have on the six streams of thought.

Defining the thought streams in future terms causes a GENERALIZATION and/or ABSTRACTION of the thought streams, which aids in synthesis of the six streams to two streams. At this point there should be sensed a lift to a higher perspective, where things and modes and thought streams should be seen anew.

The impact upon the future(s) and/or model(s) in this synthesis level, could be called VISIONING or RE-VISIONING. One should be on the verge of a synergy of all the thought streams at this point, in the expanding spiral of futurlogics.

Three futures together may be seen as:

TIMELINE CONNECTED:

We channel through the absolute future, natural future, paradigm future to the vision of the new knowledge. (Channeling as it is used in this sense is defined as, "to use one's intuition.")

Also three futures together may be seen as:

INTELLIGENCE CONNECTED LEVELS:

We channel through the imaginary future, artificial future, synthetic future to the vision of the new knowledge. (Channeling as it is used in this sense is defined as, "to use one's insight.")

This should bring us to the FUTURLOGICS **DMP** which is defined as follows:

DMP is the central action principle of VISIONING. Remember **DMP** is cycle free, mode free thinking. (**DMP** is short for holistic thinking, with insight and intuition fueling the mental synergy.)

Remember again:

- A **cycle** is a thought routine.
- A **mode** is a deductive thought routine.
- A **model** is an inductive thought routine.

This is a mode free thinking area "free lance thinking" to generate a MENTAL VISION of "where it is all going?" in our considerations and pondering.

(Note: we consider with our minds and ponder with our hearts.)

(Modal thinking is a method of thinking that ignores the other methods, and is very focused in using this method exclusively. It is deductive reasoning. This is a form of analysis.)

(Model thinking is a method of thinking that synthesizes the other methods into its method. It is characterized by much unlearning, as new things are introduced. And is very open to using this method inclusively. It is inductive reasoning. Model thinking can be called channeling)

DMP

Futurlogics is a system, we can re-loop through in multiple cycles, to produce the expanding spiral of thought, that is the Futurlogics final method/principle or **DMP**.

All of Futurlogics is founded upon these two axioms:

Truth is knowledge of things as they are, and as they were, and as they are to come;
Intelligence is light (software of the mind) and truth.

Intelligence is equivalent to the Futurlogics **DMP**.

These are Futurlogics modes of **truth**:

- **Absolute Mode** (knowledge of things as they were,)
- **Natural Mode** (knowledge of things as they are,)
- **Paradigm Mode** and **Model** (knowledge of things as they are to come.)

These are Futurlogics modes of **light**:

- **Imagination Mode** (Power of imagination,)
- **Artificial Mode** (Assumptive / Transforming substitutions,)
- **Synthetic Mode/Model** (Creative forces/ Power.)

These six thought streams are all directed to one end which is **DMP**. **DMP** is a dual acronym disassembled or decoded next:

(D)irect (M)ind (P)erception and (D)irect (M)ental (P)rocess.

There are six modes/models (streams/perspectives) in Futurlogics.

(D)irect (M)ind (P)erception represents enlightenment in consciousness.
(D)irect (M)ental (P)rocess represents reasoning in truth.

Everything is directed to **DMP** in the Futurlogics system as the Pyramid Paradigm portrays on the next page:

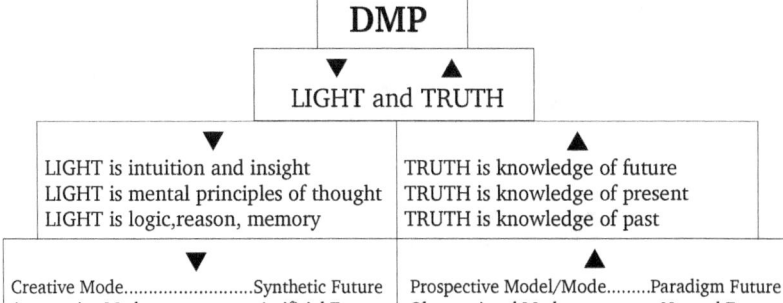

Without light there is not truth but knowledge only.
Without truth there is no light but darkness.
Intelligence is Light and truth.
DMP is Native Intelligence

The six fundamental internal mental operations central to developing **DMP**,or Direct Mind Perception/Direct Mental Process are the balance between:

● CROSS MODE MASKING,

● COMPENSATION ,

● HEURISTICS,

● JUDGMENT,

● CREATIVITY,

● KNOWLEDGE

These components are needed to use the whole mind, and are defined on the next page:

● *CROSS MODE MASKING* is the affect from channel or sense blaring, that dominate other inputs, so as to cause an attenuation, or blocking, or mode/cycle style of thought, to the other inputs. The opposite of cross mode masking is compensation. Example, sight dominates the inputs the other senses send. Or sometimes a sound is so loud we loose the ability to see clearly.

● *COMPENSATION* is the heightened thought and sensory awareness, and sensitivity due to a blockage of one channel, or sense, or thought. Example, the blind using all his other remaining senses, to make up for the loss of his sight, will illustrate this effect.

● *HEURISTICS* is the happy discoveries made without logical or patterned thought. It is the improvements made to the mind, because the mind finds new ways to do things, in a "shorthand" fashion. It says, "if it works for me, I'll use it", even if it cannot be explained, or if it comes out of the blue, or if it has a self contained logic of its own—because it works!

● *JUDGMENT* is the ability to evaluate incomplete data, partial information or imperfect knowledge.

● *CREATIVITY* is synthetic thought that combines, builds, adds, to get a new idea or new approach.

● *KNOWLEDGE* is our awakening to existence.

The future in FUTURLOGICS is used as a provocation to thought, and as a leveler to dogma and academic impedance to new thought and ideas. The future as total abstraction, develops the mind to deal with things which are purely mental and only subject to reason and intuition. It is a natural "brain storm." And finally, the future is a short reference to all the things and events that we have yet to learn and experience—it is the frontier of the mind. Everywhere future is mentioned, think of the unknown or the horizon of our research.

FUTURLOGICS BASIC COMPONENTS

00.	PARADIGM MODEL	(PARADIGM LIFT)
0.	PARADIGM MODE	(PARADIGM SHIFT)
1.	CREATIVE MODEL	(SPIRITUAL CREATION)
2.	ASSUMPTIVE MODEL	(LAY HOLD AND ACT UPON)(FAITH)
3.	IMAGINARY MODEL	(INSPIRED IMAGINATION)
4.	NATURAL MODEL	(GOD'S PRESENT or IDEAL PRESENT)
5.	ABSOLUTE MODEL	(PAST) (INFINITE HISTORY)
6.	CREATIVE MODE	(TEMPORAL CREATION)
7.	ASSUMPTIVE MODE	(FIGURATIVE ACTING OUT OF IMAGINATION)
8.	IMAGINARY MODE	(MAN'S IMAGINATION)
9.	NATURAL MODE	(OBSERVABLE NOW THROUGH SENSES)
10.	ABSOLUTE MODE	(HISTORY ACCORDING TO MAN)

FUTURLOGICS PARTNERS OR THOUGHT STREAMS:

PARADIGM FUTURE:

| 00. | PARADIGM MODEL | Paradigm Lift, View/Vision |
| 0. | PARADIGM MODE | Paradigm Shift |

SYNTHETIC FUTURE :

| 1. | CREATIVE MODEL | Theoretical Creation |
| 6. | CREATIVE MODE | Actual Creation |

ARTIFICIAL FUTURE :

| 2. | ASSUMPTIVE MODEL | Action To Make Real, Faith/Substitute Model |
| 7. | ASSUMPTIVE MODE | Action To Facilitate Action |

IMAGINARY FUTURE :

| 3. | IMAGINARY MODEL | Imagine The Real |
| 8. | IMAGINARY MODE | Imagine The Unreal |

NATURAL FUTURE :

| 4. | NATURAL MODEL | Cosmos At Present Includes Dark Matter |
| 9. | NATURAL MODE | Observable Now |

ABSOLUTE FUTURE :

| 5. | ABSOLUTE MODEL | Cosmic History Or The Past |
| 10. | ABSOLUTE MODE | History According To Man |

Training the mind, to capture and preserve first impressions, can be very useful to creativity, insight, intuition. First impressions, if not protected can be mutated, by thinking that does not respect inspiration.

Study Subjects for the Future-minded in the Paradigm Future.

- *Love of Truth.*
- *Love of Knowledge.*
- *Amount of Knowledge.*
- *Strength of Consciousness enables Futuring the Future.*
- *Diligence, Persistence, Perseverance.*
- *Prediction, Foretelling, Prophecy.*
- *Beware of False Certainty.*

PART THREE

APPLICATION

(ALL ACTIVITIES WHEN INTERNALIZED BECOME PRINCIPLES)

Chapter X

PREDICTION

ACTIVITIES RELATIVE TO THE FUTURE:
PREDICTION, FORETELLING, PROPHECY

Before we get into a discussion of the general theory, terms must be defined. Generally speaking, the term prediction can be used for all the prognostication we do. We will emphasize certain aspects of the prognosticating process with a separate and distinct term. However, prediction, foretelling and prophecy will generally mean the same thing (loosely defined), and for most practical purposes they can be used interchangeably.

When the term *prediction* is used, we stress the conscious aspects of the forecasting process. Prediction is the mental processes normal introspection of the forecasting efforts would reveal, upon conscious reflection. Do not think prediction does not use subconscious thought, or that intuitive and insightful processes might not be present and operating. Prediction is merely a shortened reference to the conscious aspect of forecasting and prognostication.

Foretelling might then be used to represent and accentuate the subconscious factors and operations in the forecasting process. Although prediction and foretelling are essentially the same, when we mention foretelling as a special prescience, we will stress a feature of the forecasting process. Foretelling then is suggestive of the subconscious means to view the future. Foretelling in its special sense, de-emphasized the conscious and logical processes. Foretelling involves what may be called "gut feel" or hunches.

Prophecy is used to classify that region of mental activity beyond the normal operations of the mind. Prophecy suggest that the mind is assisted by higher or extraordinary powers or perceptions. The tenor of most religious principles are present in the prophetic approach.

With few exceptions these classifications will be used to allude to these special features.

PREDICTION WITH A MODE

The six modes individually will all produce a future, if they are used to the exclusion of the futurlogical method which allows modeling and **DMP**. The difference is the distortion or incompleteness of the future obtained through the use of a specific mode exclusively. This is because by definition, the previous knowledge or pattern of approach will overlay and influence succeeding knowledge. That is the retrospective mode will produce a future that is characteristic of the absolute future. Also the observational mode will produce a future that is profiled as the natural future, the imaginative mode will have imaginative content remaining, the substitute mode or the assumptive mode will be actionable notions of the future that may or may not be true, the creative mode where plans and preparation build a future, and the prospective approach where the mode can be a model and visa versa.

The most accurate prediction then would logically be to avoid the use of only one method of obtaining data/information. But before we can avoid the using of a particular mode, we have to be conscious of that mode, from outside that mode. This will require metacognition and other modes. We should then determine the tendency we have to depend on particular patterns of thinking, inherent to particular modes. When we can think in all the patterns of approach, then we will get a "feel" for Futurlogics and the action of **DMP**, in prediction and thinking of the future in general. Then paradigms can shift, and lift, and be like gifts.

This does not imply that the future produced by the mode(s) is not partly true. It is true in some degree, history will repeat itself. Trends will and can play out. Imagining the future will bear fruit. Assuming a future is a beginning of making the future as we want it to be. And to a large degree, we can direct and create our own future. Nevertheless, we must be aware of the limitations of each mode and not forget there may be other ways.

THE SIX MODES ARE THE RESULT OF
SUBCONSCIOUS FORETELLING

Each of the favorite modes that have been discussed is the product of subconscious process, originating from a cycle which has organic origins such as: memory, senses, imagination, motives, hand/ mind power to make tools, finally consciousness of consciousness and metcognition. Even though the modes may have begun as a conscious process through constant use, they become habits, so that finally an approach which began without any awareness of the other ways of approaching the future, becomes ingrained and the other ways are discounted.

Since foretelling in such a limited fashion, through any one particular mode will not produce a complete picture of the future, which is essential to prediction, foretelling or prophecy by the futurlogical method. The affect/effect of the narrow modal approaches must be brought to consciousness. From this conscious awareness of the modes, we can then expand to prediction through all the modes simultaneously in synergy. This at first, is a conscious effort fraught with excessive logical thought and conscious manipulation of the modes, but through constant practice it will eventually bring the process and system to the subconscious habit. When this happens, we set the stage for subconscious processes using all the modes in a futurlogical means. Foretelling through Futurlogics then is an automatic operation which makes **DMP** contact with the future possible.

Futurlogics begins as a conscious system of prediction, but as it becomes habitual it proceeds to a subconscious transition of foretelling— which is the beginning of **DMP**. Once **DMP** is experienced, then the only better way of learning of the future is through the high-altitude method of prophesy.

Prediction through the Futurlogical approach expands perception and produces a clear discernment of the imaginary and artificial contents, which are the sources of false notions of the future. Becoming especially aware of what is imaginary and what is artificially accepted as a "future," we then can see clearly what is *not* the actual future. Prediction or foretelling, if they do not show us the actual future are of no practical use, but are only mental exercise.

TWO KINDS OF PREDICTION

Organization and definition might be an additional help to clarify some general properties of prediction patterns. The future can be described and studied without the reference to time and place. This type of prediction might be called "general" since no demands are placed upon the events and conditions that are forecast. The other type of prediction pattern is the opposite. We demand that the time and place of the event and condition be known, or "specific" information be given. *Specific prediction* is intended to discover and know the time and location of events, places, and conditions within some future frame. In *general prediction*, we state the facts and laws of ulterior reality, i.e. futurity; this is done without mention of specific time or place. For example: "All persons will grow, age, and die," or "Life will be discovered in some solar system of our galaxy." In each of these predictions no time or specific place is mentioned yet they are statements of the future. General predictions describe conditions and elements of futurity.

Examples of specific prediction are: "It will rain in the downtown area a ten o'clock tomorrow morning," and "By the years 2000, the governments of the earth will be centralized and headquartered in the state of Missouri," etc.

We can see the relationship of general and specific prediction by the following analogy: when a sculpture is undertaken, the general shape of the stone is analyzed. Then the outline of the form is cut into the stone. Once this foundation is formed and hewn out of the stone, then details are delicately chipped in and the finishing touches are polished away. General prediction is the rough stone that outlines the main structures of the eventual statue. We cannot sculpt a rock without making the large cuts that break the stone to the rough form, that will finally be refined by progressive action of chipping and polishing.

IMPROVING WHAT WE CAN ALREADY DO

Here is a list of predictive techniques that is already done. There is more than what are listed next, but those shown are illustrative and exemplary:

Location Prediction: Prediction over a specific area, rather than all the earth. The Earth is sectioned out by continents, countries, geographic areas, Oceans etc..

Trend Analysis: Is the extrapolation of trends or linear events in the present to the future, to generate a future line. But future curves may also be observed in social phenomena. Basic trend extrapolation is a projection of current conditions. Since some projections would be curves rather than linear extensions, be aware some curves may be "S" shaped, meaning they will bend out of "line of sight." Best for short range prediction. (Typical of the Natural Future)

Trend Synthesis: A method to get overall effect of many trends or events. This is equivalent to a macro-view of Futurlogics method/model. (Again typical of the Natural Future.)

Environmental Scanning: Gathering data in a neutral fashion as with scientific detachment, generally associative to a notional future, or just related by either cause or result. Selecting information with rules to collect data. Method to handle large data banks.

Spectrum Gradient: Setting forth hierarchical relationship with a commonality. Any objective that is separated by degrees, levels of severity, or gradients of intelligence. Valuing data points.

Opening Curtains: "Break out" events or "break through" speculations with timing. Example 'What if gasoline is replaced? Who is to lose from this discovery? Who is to gain from this discovery?' Anticipating technological breakthroughs. Paradigm shifts possible.

Scenarios: Imaginative stories about the future that have some drive or passion or consequence. Essentially the Imaginary Future that is based on conscious rather than subconscious assumptions. (Typical of the Imaginary Future.)

Denouements: Endings to complex predictions, foretelling or prophecy:
  1. The final outcome of the main dramatic complication in a literary work. Note: Last Day(s) as portrayed in the scriptures.
  2. The outcome of a complex sequence of events that is *Backcasted*, to determine the cause(s) and method(s) to produce this view of the future, which is either a bellwether, pilot and/or precursor.

Visioning: Building vivid mental images and models of the future, that will be a motivating force to build or wait for the future envisioned. (Typical of the positive side of the Artificial Future.)

Delphi Conferencing: Group Futurlogics or futuristic(s) discussion as answered in these pages. But currently seen as a blind survey of the experts' portend(s) concerning future scenarios.

Cross-Impact Analysis: Part of the 'System Thinking' concepts of cycles: virtual, vicious, balanced, and their interactions.

Global Models: Due to the confinement of the Earth, there will be this demarcation of all forces and causes. (Unless religion brings in extra-earth concepts such as heaven, after-life existence, resurrection, millennium. Global government will oppose religion for this reason, because it breaks the "natural confinement" of the Earth. "They" will first establish one church. This opposition is a prediction that is easy to 'see'.)

Computer Generated Models and Simulations: Computer algorithm of real events to measure extreme and complex interactions. Used where massive data exist such as weather, earthquakes, etc..

Technological Forecasting: Part of the Natural Future or the observational mode, extrapolations and/or interpolations. Using science to predict.

Technological Assessment: Part of the Natural Future or the observational mode quantifications. Math as a predictive method— notably statistics.

Precursor or Bellwether Analysis: Using leads or living examples to predict wider scale applications. The prophet/futurist Isaiah used many local events to typify future events. (Suggestive of Paradigm Mode.)

Risk Assessment: The Artificial Future or decision impact analysis.

Cost-Benefit Analysis: Planning resource allocations. See activity of Planning in this book. Also THINKING ABOUT THE FUTURE Edited by Andy Hines and Peter Bishop © 2006. Decision advantage analysis.

Examples of Nature: The use of natural occurrences such as, animal migrations and survival in nature that portend human invention. Plant adaptations apply to the human condition. *VELCRO®* was an invention inspired by the burr in nature.

Money Trails: Following the money, creation to destruction, buying or selling, valuation to devaluation. Macroeconomic, microeconomic, economic forecasting, etc..

Authoritative Pronouncements: Predicting dogma as a form of social conditioning. Manufactured consent etc..

Weather and Geophysical Events: The effect/affect of the Earth and it's movements and moods, to influence or change the living conditions of man on this planet.

Religion and Cultural Influences: Man's beliefs and man's traditions, in conditioning and shaping the social environment of man.

Fulfillment of predictions in principle vs. Fulfillment of predictions in actuality: Theory vs. practice.

Not Here Method: When confronted with a vast list of possibilities and even probabilities, this technique takes one item in the list and determines if it is in "this place?," or if it is in "that place?," or "is it here?" or "is it there?". After this the prognosticator concentrates his efforts, to pare down the list, to "maybe here?" or "not here?" search. The purpose of this technique is to reduce big list to a little list.

Personal Outcome: Prediction of internal mental and emotional changes that are not visible externally, but can be reported to the investigator by testimony/response.

Fulfillment of historical levels of Societal Progress as seen by Man:

    1. Hunter/Gather Level

    2. Agricultural Level

    3. Industrial Level

    4. Communication Level

    5. Knowledge Level

    6. Thinking Level

    7. Spiritual Level

Many use, if not engineer, society to conform to the above progress level of man's social progress.

We predict in one way or another! The fact that we know there is a future proves that we have done some general prediction. (There are many subjects in the study of mathematics that concern probabilities and chance, evaluated in a quantitative manner. We are not going to reiterate in detail all the techniques and tools just listed above, as there are many books written on these technique of evaluating the future.) Our purpose here is to reinforce the idea that we can all predict in one fashion or another, and sometimes, these predictions are perfected to the degree of a science. Indeed, the scientific method is designed to certify the cause-effect relationship of natural phenomena, so that when a given condition is encountered, the effect can be anticipated.

Our present abilities can be improved. Prescience and foreknowledge can and must be thought of as a possible goal. However, the existing bank of knowledge always seems to be accompanied by its own survival instincts. It tries to maintain the status quo. We fight against change almost as instinctively. Learning new things means change, therefore improving our present abilities to look ahead and forecast will be similarly blocked. By now, we should be able to learn new patterns of thought. The modes we have discussed are the examples of old ways that will prevent or distort new views.

Before we can improve, we should know where we are now. If in doubt, start somewhere and call it the beginning, in the temporal environment any point can be defined as a beginning. It is suggested to then write our beliefs of the future. This can be written in one sitting, or from notes accumulated over a period. The main thing is to begin as accuracy is optional, for it is difficult to operate from a vacuum basis. After general statements concerning the future are made, we can make specific references to events we know will happen. At this point, we are not too concerned with the validity of the predictions. We are simply "beginning the game" and "getting the ball rolling." Reserving our negative thoughts should keep us from becoming mired in doubts.

Now that we have something to work with, we can put things into the true, false and "needs more thinking category." Obviously, some things will feel "far out" and others will be self-evidently true, but getting too wrapped up in judgments of truth will hamper the free-flow of thought. We will pursue this effect when we discuss other techniques.

UPDATING AND REVISING

This working or prototype future can be looked upon as a starting place. Prediction in this sense takes on the form of updating and revision. We take this future and change it and add to it until, we have the ideal mode of Futurlogics. This process brings us to the best level of "foreknowledge" we could achieve.

The principle of updating and revising is, that of adding to our real future, discovering our artificial future, mapping out the imaginary future, learning to distinguish the absolute, natural, and the synthetic futures. In short, it focuses the vague notions we have into concrete workable designs. Even actionable future(s).

Updating comes from the new things we learn that add to our present foreknowledge. As we grow in the *art of futurlogics*, updating should be expected on a regular basis. Updating does not correct past assumptions, but its emphasis is upon expanding and enlarging.

Revision suggest the result of a discovered error or the discovery of better methods. Many times when we find wrong information, we then revise our plan or change our mode of operation to fit the new look. This means that, it is a change of "future" which cause our realization of error or inconsistencies. Therefore, revision differs from updating in that it does more than add—it corrects false percepts. In the words of the modes, it separates the real from the unreal.

MODES: FUTURLOGICS: PREDICTION

The "futures" work in varying degrees within us. By deciding which of these futures come from predominant modes, we can get a better understanding of ourselves and the frame of reference we use, to foretell and predict. Our theories of the future, simply will be like a frame to our study. The modes limit and channel our inquiries. Futurlogics is the ability to free-float these modes, so that we do not settle on one or two narrow perspectives, thus making diverse foretelling or prediction impossible. The varieties and hues possible through combinations of modes is easily seen, as we become more detached from any one mode and think in overall Futurlogics' mode, which points us toward the true future.

Whatever our position, we will interpret data to support our primary view. When we set out to learn the workings of the universe we relate it to our lives or we describe it in the parameters of ourselves. To ourselves, we are the most important thing in the universe; therefore, we pay attention in terms of ourselves. It is most difficult to express the phenomena of nature directly. We use language and terminology with which we are already familiar, to describe the previously unknown. **DMP** and Futurlogics puts us in direct contact with the future, so we will think of the future in terms of the future.

CHANGING GENERAL PREDICTION TO
SPECIFIC PREDICTION

General prediction is prescience without reference to time or place. Specific prediction uses both time and place as their main emphasis. The future is infinite. There are no limits to time and space. It staggers the mind to look at all places, at all future(s), at all time at once. If time and the future have no natural demarcations and topology, then we must make them, in order to apply our thought process to it.

Time and place have natural cycles and locations. Days, months, years, etc. are time periods that come from describing the phenomena of nature. Place is located because we are confined to the Earth and this solar system at the present—except for the rare excursions of astronauts. These circumstances are inherent to the physical environment. These natural demarcations point our mind to the future of the planet Earth, and some particular time span like a year or a century.

The future of the planet, or even a continent on the planet, may not be specific enough for the average person to utilize in his daily life. Yes, the future must be useful and practical. Therefore, we assign limits of convenient time and place. Anyone using a map, must find landmarks and reference points to correlate with the map. We first find out where we are, then where we are going, and finally the best route to get there. Prediction is the same, we should realize where we are, then to what time frame we have reference, and then we work to discover where we will see the event occurring.

The more advanced our civilization is, the greater is our need for time measurement and place measurement. Everyone carries a watch. Also, everyone has an address from which to base operations. Even if home is the entire city, there is an address for communication purposes.

How specific our predictions should become is the test of how much the predictions will fit into our daily routine. But some general predictions can also influence daily activity. The point is that the future can be broken up to provide us with an analytical approach. Subconscious foretelling however, will be hampered by exact time and place, as subconscious processes often work independently of temporal reality. But the zone of attention can be channeled, and therefore our subconscious will be directed through this means. (Incidentally, there are certain biologically-timed events that influence our subconscious and finally our conscious moods, that will add to the possible selection of prediction periods.) When we restrict conscious prediction, we also affect the zone of subconscious foretelling.

Before a concentrated attempt at specific prediction, it is advised that we obtain groundwork in the general form of foretelling and prediction. This is not a strict rule but a suggestion. A bank of general foreknowledge from which to judge specific prediction is desirable. The point is to get started and roll the ball out.

Each person should find the technique to fits individual personality and needs. What works well for one person may confuse another. This is especially true when we consider that each of us may favor a certain mode, a particular style individual to their personality.

SUGGESTIONS THAT MAY IMPROVE
PREDICTIVE ABILITIES

We cannot improve what we do not try. Exercising the methods we use now will be a beginning. It might be best to take notes in a log book especially dedicated for the purpose of comparing the gained objectivity in the technique, and thus discern the mode that dominates our concept of the future. A futures book if you will.

☐ 1. Spare moments offer a chance to scan ahead current events and to orient ourselves to the time necessary to predict. This is also a time when the subconscious mind is free to problem-solving and can be more easily tapped and used. Prediction is best in a relaxed state.

☐ 2. Learn the words that express future tense so that notes can be described correctly.

☐ 3. Watch how people refer to future events, and how they express themselves to gain certainty or "feeling" for oncoming events.

☐ 4. Periodically guess at things where minimal risk is involved to keep the mind active in prospective thought. One need not broadcast guesses to avoid ridicule from others. Many a guess has led to sure foreknowledge, as subsequent events proved intuitive insights.

☐ 5. Try to free the predictions from specifics and get the most general meaning and description. This prevents the prediction from becoming a self-sustaining mode that is a deductive thought chain. Use similes and metaphors to express the prediction. The literature of the Bible is at its most powerful, when parallel thought is used to express meaning. The greatest effort of prospective thought is found in the Bible, and it should not surprise us that there are verbal arts involved in these exercises that generalize our thoughts.

☐ 6. Use the techniques of brainstorming to break up rigid patterns of thought that block clear thinking. Start with the wildest flights of fancy first, then work toward the concrete and practical. Brainstorming techniques can bring to consciousness many subconscious ideas, which facilitate the art of foretelling, particularly of an artificial future. Reserve criticism to a specified time and place.

❐ 7. Trace the source of your thoughts to organic origins if you can, to see if the ideas come from "within" or "without." ESP and **DMP** may be found to be real factors in your insights, and if so, being able to discern where the idea began may be a valuable clue to "contact" with futurity. Remember that no one has yet disproved this awareness. To those who know of the reality of such things, trying to explain them to one who denies their existence is like describing color to a blind man.

❐ 8. Wait for different moods to balance the effect that emotions play in prediction. Moods are important, because they influence the content of our thoughts.

❐ 9. Assume a different role in society. Our self-concept has much to do with the direction our thoughts take. Identification with strong religious or political figures will influence our interests in special aspects of the future, which if we identify with a condemned murderer for instance, we may never consider. We change our opinions of ourselves with each new mood. Therefore self-image is another dimension of **DMP**. Self-esteem is very valuable to the future-minded.

❐ 10. Do not let immediate circumstances overpower you to see things in terms of the moment. During times of prosperity people tend to see the future as prosperous. During difficult times people tend to see the doom of days to come and are pessimistic. Try to break from these overwhelming inputs of environment. Keep your head above water so you can see which way you are swimming. Don't let yourself drown in the momentary. Integrity of mind regardless of circumstances.

❐ 11. Respect others so that it will be easy to accept the self you will become. If you are tolerant with others then you will be tolerant with your potential self. We hope to be able to admire the person we will become. Be good to yourself and do things now to make it easier for you in the future. Negative procrastination will alienate you from your potential self. Sacrificing now can make things easier for you later.

❐ 12. Study the source and origin of all information that you come across to be able to validate your predictions. Trust but verify.

❐ 13. Believe in yourself. If we have doubts we set up internal blocks that will "verify" the doubts. Belief *deliberates* our mental capacities. We find that using our bodies is easy as we learn to walk and function in the physical surroundings. It only takes a few years. It may take the rest or our lives to learn to use the greater percentage of our mental capacity. It is worth it.

Essential here is that if we can learn to believe in our abilities; that in itself frees latent abilities "within," that are inherent but undeveloped. Any growth of hidden talent should first begin with belief.

Every belief has its negative side: doubt. If you believe you will succeed, then at the same time you doubt that you will fail. Belief and doubt are two sides of the same coin. In this operation of belief-doubt we should be aware, which side of the coin we seem always to call. Pessimism, skepticism, and negativism form attitudes that will stultify the natural operations of the mind. We should approach prediction with a positive attitude for maximum results.

The future is an abstraction. The only contact we have with it until it happens is mental. It has no physical basis that we can experience in the usual ways. The future is experienced in the same manner in which an abstraction is experienced, and that is within the mind. The acronym **DMP** is the "contact" we want to finally achieve. **DMP** through Futurlogics, is the ideal experience mode for the future, and it is the best predictive technique. But we have to grow into this thought process. As with other thought processes, it takes time to learn. It will take the whole heart and mind of man to search ahead and to come to terms with futurity. We really should gain self-confidence.

Imagination is useful to **DMP** as it is the most natural avenue to the conscious mind of the strange, unusual, atypical or anomalous ideas. Logic and reason are based on present circumstances and observations. The future is often seemingly irrelevant to immediate surroundings. By/through imagination the unexpected or the unthinkable can be envisioned. The imaginative processes can extend beyond the routine and mundane influences to five new perspectives/modes. We cannot experience the future physically, but we can simulate it by the imaginative process. Imagination is the screen upon which we can, with **DMP** view the future. Creative imagination will be essential to a study of the future and its ulterior reality.

The believing mind will naturally have a more flexible imagination. Imaginative creativity is a strong stimulus to future thinking. It is a breath of fresh air. To be skeptical and to regiment the imagination is to thwart progressive growth and learning.

Modes and mental blocks, which if they do not prevent free thought will certainly modify it and are the extreme examples of the inhibitions of the mental attitudes upon learning.

THE PARADIGM MODEL VS. THE PARADIGM MODE

The paradigm mode is exceptional because it can also become a model, from which knowledge of the future patterns subsequent knowledge. As we successfully obtain information of/about the future through Futurlogics and **DMP,** the knowledge gained helps us discern and further foreknowledge. This is the model effect of this mode and its more "perfect" than the others. A greater amount of knowledge of the future can be obtained. The only time the paradigm approach is a mode is when there is very little knowledge, or when that knowledge is highly specialized, as when knowledge of the extreme distant future is used to determine the immediate or the known future is used to determine the far distant future.

The more we know for certain the more we can know. Foreknowledge is the yeast in the bread dough. Foreknowledge is certain knowledge, and it will serve as a basis upon which we will collect insights and mind-expanding **DMP** experiences. **DMP** uses existing knowledge to absorb and collect new knowledge in a form that builds forethought. This is to be seen as a tool that builds a forward-looking mind. Simply thinking about the future may not be enough. We should grasp on to new things because they will expand our minds, and cause the next law to operate: *the more we know, the more we can know.*

OVERCOMING PITFALLS AND BLOCKS

The past has greater inertia and it will tend to make the new become old and familiar very quickly. It seems impossible to view everything new, as a child who has less past to draw upon, but we should learn to do this so that the future is not described overpoweringly in terms of the past. Children do not worry about the future, naturally following the admonition that we should "take no thought for the morrow, for the morrow will take thought for itself." We should be childlike, looking positively ahead. The attitude of prediction should be positive to prevent depression which blocks the free-flow of thought. Because of their unbiased attitudes, children learn more in the first few years of life than they will throughout their adult lives.

Man is not only aware of his life before death, but can contemplate many things beyond his own life span. It is common for grandparents to plan for the futures of their great grandchildren. Some consider and predict things beyond their lifespan. Because most of us do not know the exact date of our death. One mind-expanding technique in thinking of the future is to come to positive terms with death. We should think beyond mere selfish survival. Thinking of a future far distant to our own survival will expand and enrich everything we do now. Thinking only within the limits of our life span will restrict clear-headed prediction. Things we do or say now may be an influence for many years beyond our life span.

The mind of man can view all things because it holds simultaneously the past, present, and future. Life consist of hope, faith and an abundance given to others freely. Life can be ten thousand years long, if we can add this dimension through a vivid foretaste of the future. Instead of ignoring the future because it may hold unpleasantness, look beyond to better days. It would be no surprise to find out that the optimist thinks farther into the future than the pessimist. The future should be motivating, not depressing. Besides, being prepared makes life safer—if not possible.

FORWARD THINKING

The forward-thinking mind should be the goal of all persons who wish to develop their entire mind. As paradoxical as it is, the conscious logical process is a block to prediction, unless the system of Futurlogics is used. Since the future is often a new and different thing, the best way to face it is through the intuitive faculties we possess. In ancient times the prophets were students of dreams and visions. The dream is known to reflect the operations of the subconscious mind. Yet conscious logical thought is also a product of the subconscious mind. But no one knows completely how the mind works; therefore, ALL mental processes are below conscious investigation, except through metacognition and **DMP**. We are consciously aware of only a fraction of what the mind is doing, thus the major obstacle to thinking about the future is the lack of knowledge of how we think.

Regardless of how scant our knowledge of mental things is, this is no excuse for not doing something. On the contrary, it should be an incentive to learn at a pace that will fill this void of knowledge. We have to go ahead, even with inadequate knowledge. In this respect, the artificial future is better than no future at all; we then can view our assumptions of the future as an *experiment and a learning technique.* Standing still is no way to use the mind. It is better to begin than to wait.

We venture assumptions concerning the future to make continuous our thoughts. We cannot avoid it. Most of our assumptions come from foretelling, therefore understanding our assumptions gives us a good idea of the nature of foretelling and its subconscious workings. We are reminded again of the man who exclaimed that he best handled the problems of the future by "just not thinking of it." He doesn't consciously consider the future and considers it illogical to do so, because of its intangible nature. This is saying, subconscious means can work with the seeming contradiction of the future with the present.

This does not mean that we can't consciously consider the future, but that we should be aware of side effects and built-in obstacles. We can operate all day long on the unconscious prescience and not notice excessive doubt or perplexity. But subject our behavior to conscious thought and the demands of objective certainty, and we will experience the limits of certainty or doubt. We may not think of the future in order to remain "certain" as action requires distinct accuracy. Much like the ostrich hides his head thinking he is hiding.

The sun will shine, the earth will continue to orbit, the planet will still support normal life, these and other predictions are stock foretelling. They are taken for granted. They are assumed to continue to occur. There is no way we can prove absolutely that the sun will shine tomorrow. We accept that the rules of certainty will apply, and what worked in the past will also work for the future. As long as we don't consciously think of the unconscious prescience, they are as good as absolute certainties—because we never **_DOUBT_** them. In other words, "what you don't know won't hurt you."

Here is the reason some persons refuse to study or think of the future: as long as their prescience is not consciously thought, they are secure and certain however false their security is! Conscious analysis of the assumptions and unconscious prescience of the future, throws them into a spin of doubt and hesitation that will stultify action.

Be believing or develop a new kind of logic or proof. Learning how to prove the eventual reality of an occurrence or an event of the future, is a problem that should be dealt with. We are raised in a past-oriented culture. We have to use prospective thought process, instead of the retrospective forms which surround us. Historical perspective is overpowering if not understood.

Most of us do foretelling at the unconscious level of thought. We take it for granted and do not realize, it is prediction. We do not recognize conscious efforts to make statements about the future. We are accustomed to the fact that we live in a temporal environment and we do not see or we ignore our prescience. Yet our plans and preparations are based on a few conscious predictions, and numerous subconscious assumptions, if not prescience or foretelling.

When we consciously predict it is often just the making ourselves aware of our unconscious prescience, and we experience disturbance or anxiety in prediction. Part of this is due to our need for certainty, distinction, security, and safety. The other reason is the subconscious nature of the origination of ideas.

We may not see our subconscious processes, but we can by inference, recognize that some assumptions and foretelling had taken place. Actions and plans are based upon a premise arrived at through mental processes, we yet do not fully understand but they really are expectations of things derived from subconscious assumptions or foretelling.

The "mental operating system" of Futurlogics guides our subconscious foretelling and makes it modal free. Therefore the accuracy of our predictions increases. **DMP** can be thought of as the subconscious thought processes, perfected by the Futurlogical system of modal free intuitive thought, and the model of insightful thinking. Futurlogics is the handy means to control our subconscious foretelling in a simple way. The obstacles in dealing with the subconscious are taken care of automatically, and **DMP** is the final result.

Chapter XI

THE PRINCIPLE OF WAITING

IMPULSE CONTROL THE ACTIVITY OF BEING STILL

There is nothing future that will not eventually become present. All of the future can be known if we simply wait and see.

Contrasted to present reality, futurity has a separation period of time between events. These periods necessitate waiting before that future reality becomes present reality. In predicting the future, we must also be aware of the waiting periods necessary before experiencing the future, as we experience present realities. The future must be waited for.

As we grow up, we gain a longer span of attention. Children have a fleeting attention span and can wait for withheld rewards for only moments. Children have to learn to be patient. Adults can in some ways, wait for rewards that extend beyond their lifetime. The ability to wait and to pay attention to facts for longer periods of time, enables us to view and learn about our future. In the discussion of the artificial future we learned, that a person's need for a future causes him to assume a future in order to facilitate present action, which suggests that if we hold off long enough before taking action, we could learn more of the true future. The greatest aid to prediction is the ability to withhold our impulses, that is stay action or "be still," to eventually know the future. Impulsive action and the constricting effect of the individual six modes will distort (if not totally block) what we could know of the future.

WAITING AND THE STIMULUS OF THE FUTURE

If a person acts from present circumstances observable to all then, what onlookers see is a natural reaction to obvious conditions. However, if one acts from some knowledge of future event(s) which are not easily seen, then his activities seem incongruous to the "obvious" conditions that prevail. An example of this is a familiar Bible account of the building of the Ark, and Noah's call to do so. Here we have a man engaged in a vast project, building a large barge which if built near an ocean would not seem strange. But the reaction of the neighborhood suggests that the nearest body of water must have been beyond practical means. Because of this, the community laughed and mocked his efforts calling Noah "crazy." From their point of view, it was natural to believe that the man and his project were deserving of their ridicule. If they had been "tuned in" to the oncoming flood as Noah was, they would have been so busy building their own arks, they wouldn't have had time to make sport of Noah. The "obvious conditions" to the average onlookers suggested that there was certainly no need for such and expensive "hobby," when a vast amount of wood was hauled in from the forest.

Are we motivated out of present stimuli or are we motivated out of an awareness of future conditions and events? (Perhaps both?) Often the best way to study the answer to this is, to view it against a backdrop or its opposite. But what is the opposite of action prompted out of the future? In order to clearly discuss these two concepts of motivation, we should define and name them. Procrastination is to put off present action for some future time. But what Noah did is the opposite—he put off his daily routine and immediate needs to embark upon his "folly." He waited until the Ark landed on the mountain top before he resumed his daily routine of living. Noah postponed, or suspended his interaction with the present, and was stimulated by the fact of a future flood.

Oftentimes we should wait awhile before we resume our regular course of activity, before responding to a future condition. We wait, meaning postponement of action on other stimuli. Waiting is like procrastination in that it defers action. However, procrastination puts off present action required for the future, and waiting defers present motivations to respond to other stimulation of the future and **DMP**. When we act upon future conditions, we wait upon present conditions. Our immediate drives and impulses are delayed so we can respond towards the future. Therefore without some degree of patience, we could not deal with the future at all. The impatient person "gives in" to the moment and will not wait, and could be subject to a *false* artificial future. The prompt person does not procrastinate, but as early as possible gets ready for the future. The prompt person prepares things long before the crush or deadline forces him to do, what could have been done long before. The prompt person acts out of a *true* artificial future or from a *vision* like Noah did.

DISPELLING THE ARTIFICIAL FUTURE

Previously discussing the artificial future, we linked the basic drives and motivations of man's behavior to generating a "future" or a substitute future. If vision motivates a man also, then this appears to contradict the above statement, if we fail to look at the reverse effect where the future acts upon our motivational system. But now if we say that our ideas and thoughts of the future, restrict and channel the motivational system. Then how do we reconcile the motivational affect of the future? Waiting implies a holding back in order to accommodate a response. If we acted only out of a stimulus-reaction behavior, we would react only to the input of our physical senses. But we act also according to our ideas of the future, experience and memory.

In the complex brain and within the consciousness of the mind of man, behavior is contingent upon what is known. Civilization is directly related to what a person knows. In the artificial future knowledge is so important to motivation that the mind will generate a substitute knowledge, to allow pent-up drives and motives, to follow their course. Even though false knowledge (or artificial knowledge) of the future delays the problems of living, until we run headlong into reality. The artificial future is an elaborate type of procrastination— procrastination because we are unable to wait for the actual future—to be motivated by it.

If we are unable to defer action, of the type stimulated by present conditions, drives, motives, then the future becomes more difficult to predict. Being able to endure expectations and anticipation is directly related, to our ability to predict and foretell the future. Therefore to gain a deep foreknowledge of the future, we have to understand the principle of waiting and deferring basic physical drives.

FOREKNOWLEDGE AND KNOWLEDGE OF THE FUTURE

Previously we have not made any sharp distinction between *knowledge of the future* and *foreknowledge*. Indeed, a sharp distinction at that stage was not necessary. But with the present discussion it is appropriate to point out the difference. Simply, foreknowledge is not mere data or information, but it embodies at the same time the *'application'* of that knowledge of the future to the present, in its definition. A knowledge of history is useless unless we can apply it to the present, it gives us **meaning**. When we can relate history to the present it becomes *experience*. Likewise, knowledge of the future when applied to the present becomes *foreknowledge*, it gives us **purpose**. This is the ultimate aim of anyone who casts himself adrift in the ocean of the future. When we combine experience or meaning and foreknowledge or purpose, we enter the dominion of wisdom. Wisdom is the ability to apply history and futurity to the present.

CONSCIENCE AND WAITING

Few of us want our impulses to get out of control. It is cool to be cool. We have learned by sad experience that to act rashly will produce unwanted results. We want to do things in an orderly and profitable manner, so that we can be successful. Organizing our behavior results in obtaining the objectives of our impulses. This paradox of restraint is largely the result of learning, from the occasional flights of wild unrestrained activities we may have experienced, that we call "mistakes." We learned eventually that we should temper our actions to prevent waste and possible danger.

Conscience like religion is a word charged with high feelings and sentiments. Self-control and its mastery is a worthy goal. We admire the people who have not only themselves under control, but who can also withstand all manner of temptations that prostitute honor for immediate sensation. Although ethics and its theory is not the purpose of this book, certain aspects of our study of the future make it necessary. This basic principle in our study of the future which is waiting, make it necessary. The principle of waiting will take into account the above ethical and moral implications of impulse control by allusion. We do this because the future acts as a modifier to our impulses and motives, much the same way as our conscience; conversely the artificial future we generate is influenced by conscience and self-control. The artificial future can be a vision or it can be a myth.

It is impossible to have self-control or conscience with out some idea of the future! The futures propounded by the world's various religions reflect this quest for control in their percepts of conscience. It is always associated. Conversely the kind of future we conceive or perceive, will qualify and define our conscience. All the various forms of self-control and moral judgment are based upon some conception of the future. If we block the future from our minds, then we paralyze our self-control and our conscience. People do not want to think of the future because it reminds them of the consequences of their actions. They become responsible. On the other hand, a "bad conscience" makes thinking ahead by prediction difficult, especially when the future touches untactfully upon areas where our conscience is sensitive.

RATIONALE FOR WAITING AND IMPULSE CONTROL

As we learn more and acquaint ourselves with Futurlogics, we begin to realize that there is a reason for impulse and motivation control. Essentially the reason we should delay action is to wait for the opportune moment when action is the most beneficial to all concerned, and it enables us to move from mode to mode as required by the research. Whatever our definition of success, we should desire to succeed. We want minimum input for maximum output. We should want the most economical means to success.

An example which illustrates this type of economy is seen in times of planting seeds in seasonal climate. If a seed is planted too soon it may result in the seed freezing before it can germinate. If a seed is planted too late, there will not be enough growing season to allow full maturity as the plant develops. Then we miss the reward of fruit or flower. Some things are not to be done until the time frame arrives that favors the contingencies which will assist the seed, or project, object, goal, purpose etc. to achieve full fruition. Timing is critical to act. When we have this full sense of timing, we will know the full meaning of the term "waiting." There are windows of opportunity.

Economy and efficiency are the guideposts along the path that waiting will take. Brute force, if applied with minimum knowledge will achieve effects, but it is doubtful that it will give desired results. The side effect(s) may be detracting to the stated goal(s). Waiting sees a constant relationship between intelligence and brute force. When brute force increases the intelligence can be diminished proportionately; likewise if intelligent application of minimum force is applied with foreknowledge, then the results are naturally accelerated without a constant surveillance of the ongoing endeavor. Pure intelligence can be a force of itself. Brute force is impulsive, and intelligence is waiting for the optimum time. Brute force is always wasteful, therefore the sign of intelligence is economy and efficiency. The waiting principle is at the core of all scheduling. Intelligence diminishes the need for brute force!

PROCRASTINATION IS AN EXCEPTION

If we wait to respond to a future requirement, then we are procrastinating. If we wait to act upon **DMP**, then we are procrastinating. If we put off needful acts, work, duties, etc., to indulge in present impulses, then we procrastinate. Waiting for the right moment to respond is good, if we do not defer needful action on important matters. Setting priorities is a form of procrastination. Procrastination is generally viewed as a fault; it is seen as detrimental to well-being. The exception is: when we are procrastinating against a premature response to motivations originating from the future, or if we are timing a present action relative to **DMP**. Then we are procrastinating for a good reason due to such things as weighed out priorities. In this case procrastination is a tool, rather than a lack of motivation to act upon the future. This is against its traditional reputation, but helps us to contrast our present study. Therefore even though it can be a positive technique, generally speaking procrastination is commonly seen as a bad habit.

Both techniques of procrastination and waiting can be worked together, to time activity relative to the present and a guide for the future. Action in harmony with survival and progress are the most fundamental of all goals. We can say that *procrastination* is deferring "long-range goals" in preference to "short-range goals," while *waiting* can be termed as a deferring of "short-range goals" to accomplish "long-range goals." Every act should be a result of **balance and timing** between **waiting and procrastination**—within the sense of futurity.

PREDICTION GENERATES THE ACTIVITY OF WAITING

By prediction we become aware of the future, and as we become aware we can see the need for waiting and not simply reacting to present stimulation. If we as human beings had no future at all, we would not wait for anything. Self restraint is a virtue that bodes of survival.

We have made the careful distinction between "knowledge of the future" and "foreknowledge." Prediction produces knowledge of the future, but to arrive at foreknowledge we should know how to apply that knowledge to the present. Waiting for answers is a discordant and anxious occupation, but true foreknowledge generates no such discordant relation with the present. When we have foreknowledge, we have no waiting. If we must wait we must do it in the form of perfect timing of activity, in order to bring about optimum results and expectations. This kind of waiting can cause **DMP** and from that, we obtain a vision of the future dispelling the false artificial future.

THREE FORMS OF WAITING

We wait to produce or we wait to experience. We can make the future or we can "wait and see." Planning and the activity of planning reduces the tension and anxiety waiting produces. Preparation and the activity of preparation reduces the tension and anticipations of waiting to experience. If we do not have foreknowledge, we then must plan, prepare and orient ourselves to meet the future. We deal with these subjects later when a more in-depth discussion will be undertaken. The important thing now is that we should understand the dividing line of control. If we have limited power and resources, then there is a point at which we stop waiting to produce, and wait to experience.

First form of waiting is planning which is organization that creates a future. *Second form of waiting* is preparation which is organizing ourselves to meet a future that we cannot change, or that we can change if we are prepared. In both of these activities we use the prudence of waiting until the time is ripe, for our desires and hopes to be realized. The *third form of waiting* is to predict, foretell or prophesy to prevent the generation of a fake artificial future. So we can either wait and experience the future, or we can wait through Futurlogics for **DMP**. This third form may be termed—**Visioning**.

PERCEPTIONS OF IMMEDIATE REALITY

Perception of immediate reality is modified by the different conceptions of the future, such as might be encountered in the artificial mode. Previously we were cautioned that these conditions might affect our perception of the future. Immediate circumstances tend to color our attitude and perspective with bias. Usually what is around us is what we think about, and what we think about is what we use as parameters of thinking about the future. Essentially, this is what was propounded in the natural future or the observational mode. It leads us to interpret the future in like terms—the future is seen in the same tone and color as the conditions of the moment. **DMP** allows us to see ahead as directly as possible without the distortion of a mode. **DMP** isolates from present influences the terms of the future itself, so that the intuitive parameters of the future are the descriptive language of the future itself. Foreknowledge can inform what we see in the immediate reality.

The future we know or believe will and can affect our percept of futurity. Only pure **DMP** will bypass this effect. We may experience some preliminary distortion of the future with imperfect **DMP**, but the ideal should be sought. If the future is seen as Utopian, then we have the necessity to endure the present. The lure of future bliss draws us, making the present an obstacle to achieving the hoped for "Golden Age." The opposite future is a holocaust of doom. This outlook causes the present to be extolled. Here we are distracted from the unpleasant future by the importance of immediate things. We enjoy everything within sensory limits. The moment is savored and the future ignored, "Eat, drink and be merry, for tomorrow we die" becomes the watch-word. What we view of the future shapes and modifies our perception of the present. It set our attitude(s). It guides our senses.

These are both extreme views. A grading of slighter degree may be more suitable. The general rule however is instructive. If we are Utopian, then we look at life in a detached manner. The immediate is endured because of the comparative effect of seeing the present, against the backdrop of the glittering future. On the other hand, if the doom ahead causes the moment to be accentuated, the future becomes an abstract for dreamers or doomsayers who preoccupy themselves with the world of "now." Such materiality is common in these days of cold wars, international distrust and terrorism used to manufacture consent.

Alternately, it will be observed that the materialistic person will deemphasize the future. Any form of waiting will be weakened because the future is not esteemed as much as is the immediate. The Utopian person who is seen as moral, having character that withholds present enjoyment so future reality will not be lost, will be enabled to wait so he may eventually enjoy the fruit of his labors. Such persons are more future minded and they may think more prospectively, than the materialists who is locked in the natural future.

Waiting then, is the activity caused because we hold values of futurity at a par to the material realities of the present. We would not wait unless we valued the future in some way. The intensity of waiting is due either to how much we actually know of the future and/or how much we value what we acknowledge the future to hold.

A knowledge of the future will motivate us either positively or negatively. Since it is impossible to act except in the present, a knowledge of the future can only modify activity towards the present. If knowledge of the future produces the tension of waiting, then the activities that relieve this are designed to either change the future, or change oneself to meet a future that cannot be changed. Preparation is an approach to the present where we are able to change ourselves, to meet unchangeable future events or conditions. Planning is the approach to change the future by systematical organization.

It is difficult to know the future without the ability to wait. Waiting is patience, impulse and appetite control, fasting, conscience— all these make prediction easier. The ability to endure "the wait" enables us to see the future in more ways than one. Vision becomes possible.

Without the ability to wait we would not be capable of switching the modes of/in Futurlogics, by alternating from one mode to another mode. Futurlogics would stop as it needs to seamlessly alternate and switch paradigms/modes, to gain perspective and to bring us to **DMP**.

DMP is at the heart of Futurlogics. Again a quick definition to help the process.

(**D**)irect (**M**)ind (**P**)erception is *Insight*.

(**D**)irect (**M**)ental (**P**)rocess is *Intuition*.

DMP is *Intelligence!*

If insight and intuition did not exist in the mind, there would be no advances or inventions or discoveries except by chance or trial and error. The intent of futurlogics is to sharpen the natural tools of insight and intuition. Since Futurlogics perfects the ability to work and use the abstract percepts and concepts, it will enable and facilitate intuition and its fraternal twin insight. Really, what ever the mind does is part of the mental operating system that Futurlogics will reboot. That is using the metaphor that the mind is a computer. Perhaps this will further aid in letting the mind understand itself.

Scheduling is an activity relative to the future, and the fact that we schedule is offer as a self-proof to the mind, that there is a future. This chapter on waiting has been a very generalize reference to the activity of scheduling. Waiting is scheduling at its most primitive state. It is the more mental operation/process rather than the more physical operation, which is found in the preparation and the planning chapters that follow.

Chapter XII

PREPARATION

ACTIVITY WITH PURPOSE

A fundamental law in physical science states that for every action there is an equal and opposite reaction. All matter in motion interacts with itself and/or adjacent material. This interaction is immediate. This law applies except in the interaction of living organisms with material or interaction with other organisms. In life, action upon material existence is prompted either by a knowledge of the future or from an instinctual motive or by volition.

The cause-effect principle is important to the concept here developed as mere existence causes things to happen. These effects of our existence are either willed or they are involuntary. When they are willed, we enter a special category of material interaction. Whenever we alter conditions and cause specific effects to occur through volition—we are preparing. Anything that causes a desired effect and is done purposely—it is preparing. When we learn to control who we are and how we do things, engineering them to specific ideas, designs or plans— we are preparing. Even if our preparedness has become habitual and below awareness. If we are alive—we are actively preparing.

As defined in the section on waiting, foreknowledge is knowing what to do with the knowledge of the future we have—using this knowledge to benefit or control the conditions which we would desire or intend to be. Perfect foreknowledge (if we should achieve the ideal) would conceivably reflect a naturally purposeful action in everything we do. We would by the natural effect of knowing how to relate with the present, do everything to cause synergy for our good. Based upon what we actually know of the future now, our purpose is not clear.

Purpose defines preparation. Without intent there can be no preparation. If we have no idea of the future, we have no design or plan. The more we know of the future, the more our acts become purposeful, if we can apply that knowledge to the present, in a practical manner. Also being prepared for the future in itself frees the mind to think further ahead, because preparation allows us more time and freedom to enable us to enjoy the fruits of our preparedness. Preparedness prepares.

THE FIRST MOTIVE OF PREPARATION IS *SURVIVAL*

The squirrel gathers nuts and the bear eats himself fat. Some biological clock triggers an instinct that impels activities essential to ready the animals for the winter. Many of the things we do to ready ourselves are as crucial. We gather the harvest, fill the store houses, can or bottle the harvest, preserve meat and fruit by drying, to meet our needs for the seasons changes. These activities are so familiar they become a routine custom. We often do not realize they are in reality preparations to survive change. But a moments reflection tells us, were we to have two winters back to back, how difficult life would be, if we had only been ready for one winter? Our formulas to meet change are so fragile, any change in the economy or the times and seasons, upsets a delicate balance. We should not let other's activities be our preparation for survival, as this could be misused. We should be self sufficient too, in case our civilization should collapse under disaster or war. If nature were not so regular and predictable, life and civilization as we now know it, would not be possible.

All preparatory action strengthens and gathers resources to meet a foreseen condition or event. In a dangerous environment most of the activities of man would be to get ready for the next test of survival. It is constant practice and exercise to strengthen and quicken the reflexes. The soldiers life exemplifies this kind of readying, with an eye single for the possible battle. To the soldier, fireman or policeman preparation and survival are the same. Their rest is to prepare.

During time of safety and comfort, is the time we should use to prepare for the day when danger and hardship come. All too often we become lax during the good times letting go the rigorous action of preparatory exercise. We tend to lose sight of the looming difficulties when at ease. Easy days are for preparation.

THE SECOND MOTIVE OF PREPARATION IS *PROGRESS*

After we gain more power over our environment we then seek to use the principle of preparation for progress. We learn how to do things which will offset or eliminate the effects of nature. After we learn to survive, we then use the techniques of preparation to advance ourselves. Through our desire to improve ourselves, we turn preparation to progressive action which enhances our standard of living. Readying ourselves for a higher civilization.

Preparation for progress requires time from our needs and survival to apply ourselves for enhancement of our lifestyle. Many students have discovered this, when they have had to "drop out" of school to earn enough money to get back into school. Unfortunately many never earn enough to return. To break the yoke of working or preparing only to meet the needs of survival is an age old problem. It has been theorized that slavery in ancient times gave freemen the time and resources to discover things that enable modern man to overcome his basic needs. A more positive theory is that man learns to produce a surplus by resorting to the techniques of specialization, which makes production more efficient and therefore overproduction could supply others who also specialized. Then, this freed man to use his resources to prepare and learn. In either case, it is necessary to have extra resources and extra time to apply the preparation activity to progress and creativity. Abundance can be applied to raise the standard of living of all in a civilized society. Abundance stolen can support tyranny. Abundance used generously can advance progress.

THE THIRD MOTIVE OF PREPARATION IS *GENEROSITY*

If we have prepared well, we shall soon see that our preparations will bring returns that enable us with the time and means to further prepare and progress. The prepared to survive shall not fear. The prepared to progress will not only overcome but excel. If we are fully prepared, we can give to others that they may be prepared in like manner. If we prepare our heart we will want to be generous.

ACCURACY IN PREDICTION
MAKES PREPARATION MORE EFFECTIVE

If we imagine the future through the retrospective mode we arrive at the absolute future. History dictates that we prepare for things which are generally perpetual and recurring, because of the rolling nature of history. No one should say that this in unnecessary, but we omit the fact that new things are happening now for which there are no precedents. Using the observational mode of the natural future confines the future to the interpolation and extrapolations of what is observed, which is restrictive. Since we cannot see or hear the future as it really is we are limited, and it is so with the rest of the modes. Trying to prepare for everything we imagine the future to hold, would soon deplete the time and means we have, thus having less to apply to progressive and creative pursuits. But if we prepare for the real future, as it is gained through the techniques of Futurlogics and **DMP**, instead of an assumed future of the artificial future, then we use our efforts of preparation in the most efficient way possible. The rewards are increased, and the increased time and resources make progress more available. Economy would prevail. We would feel to donate and give to help others.

The saying that the only thing we have to fear is fear itself makes sense, if we realize that preparing for everything we see in the imaginary future is impossible, with always limited powers and resources. Specific and accurate prediction will eliminate this all-direction type of preparation that modal future(s) will produce. If we knew the exact time a thief would break into our house, we then could have a fitting welcome for his intrusion. Since we do not know when we might expect him, we lose sleep in fear he might come tonight. We then expend time and money in preparation just-in-case. If we fear the future generally, we will need assurances to dispel the barricades which deplete our resources, and find ourselves back to the survival level of preparation. Accurate prediction makes possible progressive preparation, economical preparation—suiting it to our budget.

If we stored all the basic needs of survival such as water, food, clothing, etc., enough to last for six months, the fear that drives us to the activity of preparation only for survival can be changed. In fact, those who have done this, find that they progress more and can concentrate on activities that help them to move forward. When we are motivated to prepare by creativity instead of fear, we can use this important activity to improve and enhance our style and standard of living. Responding to only the perceived negative aspects of the future depresses growth and creativity. Having a storeroom of necessities through an artificial measure can alleviate fear and can support optimism.

Also preparation helps us predict, as it frees us from the necessary routines that bury, preventing our looking ahead. Conversely prediction helps us to prepare more effectively. Futurlogics and **DMP** should make all preparation progressive and creative. Allowing more time to plan our preparations and to prepare our plans.

PREPARATION HELPS US TO UNDERSTAND THE PRESENT

Few of us can meet sudden occurrence with instant response. In order to build reflexive speed, we have to practice the action to some cue or stimulus to ready us to meet the actual event. Practice on the piano readies us for the recital or some perfect rendition to come. Fire drills are for the possibility of real fire. The training of soldiers is to harden the civilian personality to the confusion and stress of combat. These kinds of preparations can be seen everywhere.

If a student would study his lessons in such a way that he learned everything that he could on his own, and then in class he would need only take notes of the parts he did not learn by himself, then when he gets to the lecture hall he could ignore the material he already knows and concentrate on the teacher's presentation, and could ask the questions which might ease his study difficulties. By freeing the mind from the obvious before class in his preparations, he can be more attentive to the less obvious and more difficult advanced aspects of the lesson. Proper preparation can make the mind see things that ordinarily escape on the first observation. How many of us have seen a movie the second time and seen many things, we missed in the first viewing? Anticipation through preparation increases learning. Trained observers see what is done in "plain sight," missed by the untrained.

Today as a new report flashes across our television screen we know that we will hear the follow-up newscasts for weeks to come, explaining all that the event means. It is true when something happens to us, we will then spend time to analyze and evaluate the implications of that event to our life. It seems that we cannot fully appraise the present without a time to fully absorb the relevance and impact it has. The present is understood in terms of the past, because we wait until it has solidified and passed into experience. We are retrospectively oriented and we need to look at everything as if it were past. Preparation helps us get the jump on events, so we are able to witness as trained and proficient observers. The observation is enhanced by preparation.

Today things are changing so rapidly that we cannot fully understand most of the things that happen or their implications, except in a superficially scanned form. We are in an age of specialization. Experts (doctors, scientist, professors etc.) declare what we have to take for granted to be able to utilize their knowledge. Computers take the labor out of vast computations. These machines are another kind of expert, and we take their "word" because it takes too much of our time to compute it ourselves. We believe from the surface level of experience or we spend more time than we are allowed, to relate to the new generation of machines and training programs. Besides believing what the experts tell us, we must by necessity take the alternative of preparing ourselves to be more efficient. Today we would be overwhelmed by the daily course of life if we did not prepare ourselves. Living itself can be interpreted as a form of preparation. Preparation prevents our thinking system from being overwhelmed. Preparation makes thinking possible!

STAGES OF PREPARATION

There is a natural order to the phase of preparation, and though all of them may be fused into one principle, they can also be seen as distinct and definitively separate. But, for the purpose of analysis we will break the process into component parts. Later we will study the operation as a synthesized whole. The essential elements of preparation are as follows:

❒ 1. By prediction or other means we are *informed* of the future and the events that are to come. Reflecting we realize that we have not ready resources nor the powers to meet an oncoming event. If we decide events cannot be changed then the principle of preparation is initiated.

❒ 2. To structure the preparation activities, both mental and physical, we should determine the time period allowed before the event is upon us—present. A precise statement of the amount of time will make the arrangement of preparation much easier to coordinate with present activities. How much time is there to prepare?

❒ 3. Evaluate the nature of the event or environment to come, so that the problem is not misunderstood. This encourages definitive action and thought, to generate the types of things we should do to meet and endure events that will be unchangeable, if we fail to prepare.

❒ 4. Decide, determine, assess, evaluate, etc., the kind of change suitable to meet the event. Here we review the present resources we can draw upon to begin the change. We determine the things we can change that will make a difference. We compare this to what would happen if we did/do/shall do nothing.

❒ 5. Timing—when to start the things we will do is the next step in building up to the preparation activity. Set up a schedule suitable to meet the oncoming event. Procrastination and delay caused many plans and preparations to fail. Nevertheless getting started is crucial to any activity concerning the future, since delay will bring the future to the fore where advantages of advanced warning are lost, and then it (appropriate preparation) is beyond our control. Foreknowledge is of no importance unless we are able to implement and exercise it to obtain control, cooperation in the case of dealing with people, and efficiency while there is time to effect change.

❒ 6. Monitoring and feedback, seeing the development of the preparatory activity progress according to expectations and design is next. Check for errors or changes in the goals of the total activity. Any changes will throw us back to the beginning stages of preparation—at least for reappraisal.

❒ 7. There may be raw waiting or stalled activity just before the event arrives. Examples of this are quite dramatic, as in the case of the aerospace venture with a pause for the countdown. At these times we are very conscious of the passage of time. However, this is not always the case, and a general statement can be misleading.

This is the preparatory build-up to meet future events. The more general the pattern we use to plan our preparatory activities the better, as preparation is really a mental activity. Preparation is an attitude. Specific behavior is not conducive to awareness of the full temporal environment, but specificity is necessary to implement the plan of the preparation.

Preparation can be either for the natural future or the synthetic future that comes through the activities of man. Preparing for the future we think will be, will shape the quality and effectiveness of any preparatory activity. The general phases of preparation follow through the same steps for any given future; however the feedback from any specific mode, except the general mode of Futurlogics, will be more discordant. Preparation will be positive and progressive, if we will study the Futurlogics system of prospective thought.

REASONS PREPARATION IS PROCRASTINATED

First, the more we can handle the abstract and intellectual, the more we could think prospectively, Self-discipline and intelligence make preparations more real and meaningful, because we can see the results easier. Lack of intelligence is procrastination.

Second, since it takes energy to prepare, we should then find the law of physics which tells us that for every force there exists and equal and opposite force. Sometimes we lack the resources to accomplish the object of our preparation. The poverty existence that some are forced into, makes the extra energy to face the future beyond their means.

Third, habits are a big part of everything we do. If we constantly put off preparation for tomorrow soon we find that it is a habit. We procrastinate until the reality of the event is upon us, and we then experience the sudden stress, urgency, lack of time to adequately prepare. Lack of preparation is habit forming.

Fourth, we get into the habit of putting off for tomorrow because the event is so far into the future its remoteness tempts us to say that we have "plenty of time." This suggestion to our subconscious may also start the habit we mentioned, and we could get locked into this perspective.

Fifth, Vague and poor prediction will often make the defined need of preparation diffuse and unusable. This fuzzy look at the future will stultify action and this, in itself, will produce the stall found in procrastination.

Each stage of preparation may have problems attached to it, and this is enough to prevent activity. If we see clearly the stages of preparation, we can overcome such inherent problems with less resistance.

SUMMARY

Preparation is modal thinking mainly using deductive logic, but rather than arguing from a premise, assumption, hypothetical start, guess, it proceeds to a goal, truth, fact that is in the future. It readies one for a future event.

What should we do to prepare—to be prepared? We should create a synthetic future that counteracts or engineers the natural future. Nature provides the oncoming event, and the laws of nature are central to what we should do. The synthetic future impacts upon the natural future by design. The more we know, the greater the bearing it will have on what we do and how much time we have to do it. Preparation is work, and work is subject to the laws of physics. Therefore work is the essential ingredient to preparation.

Information of/about the future is the first step. A clear view of the future enables us to more closely experience present conditions. The reverse is also true. The more we know of what is presently happening, the easier it is to see the flow of inertia of present situation(s) (trends), that is when trends of current events become apparent.

The future has a schedule and a time separation between each level/layer of ulterior reality. A significant event in the future will happen in a certain passage of time and then that event will become present and so on with each layer of the oncoming events in succession. The amount of time is the framing and limiting factor of all considerations to preparation. Obviously if there is not enough time before an event will occur, it will be impossible to prepare. The purpose of prediction, foretelling, prophecy is to eliminate sudden reality or surprises. An educated feeling for the temporal extension of reality to its ulterior forms, will make preparation definitive. When and where a thing will happen is essential to the structured preparation activity.

Preparation is work and work requires energy and force. This is the next step to the employment and to the deployment of forces and resources, to bring about change. Preparation engineers change.

UNDERSTANDING CHANGE

If brute force alone solves opposition, then brute force is all that is needed. But it solves only a few problems. Force is always limited— we always apply force with some intelligence. Also brute force applied to the intelligence of man is a cause for even greater social opposition until tyranny reigns. Seldom is brute force the best answer, as the cure is usually worse than the ailment. Technology offers a wise application of force to bring about change. Also, where people are concerned we must consider emotions and ideas. Engineering social structures is a case in point where it is obvious that brute force—or any force—will cause increasing opposition. Changing material is one thing, and changing people is something entirely different. The ratio of force to intelligence is a formula in every operation that must be considered, in the light of long range side effects and consequences.

Opposition to change is not always detrimental because it can be used as a pivot to effect changes that would not otherwise be possible. All change is met with opposition and this principle cannot be avoided, so the best thing we can do is use the opposition to further produce the desired goal. This is where intelligence is a prime factor in preparing. Indeed pure intelligence is a force with no opposition. In this respect please consider Stephen R. Covey's trim tab analogy where a small opposing rudder on the larger rudder actually assist in turning the ship.

We should be informed and be aware of opposition, and this suggests the next step—feedback. We should be able to get information about our progress toward the overall goal. Communication between the implementors for reasonable assurances of acquisition of the desired goal is necessary. This all suggests a self-consciousness of action with a cognizance of all that is ongoing.

Waiting as a step in preparation should be such that constant readiness is in the background. We should remain alert even though normal activities occur. The activities of preparation may be so absorbing that consciousness of the big picture is lost. We should develop an alarm system that will bring us to attention should the overall plan of preparation becomes out of sight. Also awareness of time in relation to future reality should not be lost.

Concentration is a way of emphasizing force, and it is also a way of diminishing intelligence in other ways. When one concentrates it is by blocking out input that is distracting, however total concentration on one thing can make us oblivious to all, but that one thing. It is a real art to know when to concentrate and when to scan the entire panorama. Sometimes we must see the forest to understand the tree, also we must understand the individual tree to really know the forest. While the Bible says that we should "take no thought for the morrow" it also says that we should be looking forward to that better day—in hope waiting for the perfect man to emerge from within us. We should balance all the phases of truth: past, present, and future or internally defined: experience, knowledge, and foreknowledge.

THE PREPARED INDIVIDUAL

We esteem the individual who has become prepared with many degrees of university certification. The training he has received should have made him ready to meet the most advanced lifestyles the future has to offer. Education is the fundamental element to preparation. We should make available for our children the best knowledge handed down to us through books. A person who has an understanding of the best books is esteemed by our culture. Democracy that cannot change God given individual rights is founded on true education. To give the government to the people requires that they be prepared to make decisions to conduct affairs of government. A constitutional republic requires an informed citizenry. We should be equipped with knowledge to meet with equanimity the future, as it emerges on the shores of time. The tides of the future are like the tides of the ocean. On the very shore we meet with the power and force of the waves. Futurlogics hopes to be the boat that takes us out beyond the shoreline to where conditions are generated. We cannot stand upon the shore. For the ocean is best known by the sailors of the deep.

With the advent and advancement of the computer, there is now time to do what man can do better than the machines and that is, really think and make good decisions. The brain of man is so flexible that it can have millions of thinking systems for every purpose. Man must really learn to think again to find his potential. Perhaps children think the way we should, and we need a reminder to get back to that natural thought process. Computers and computer modeling have given man time to think, and the winners in the competition coming in the future are the ones who are thinking best! Top Management will be equal in software and data processing as the software companies unify, so the differences will be in the companies who can **OUT THINK** their market competitors. Computers process data. People process knowledge. Foreknowledge is leverage to change the future! "Think Tanks" addressing the future will be of great use and value in the world to come. Technology that obsoletes man will not replace man's creativity. Thinking skills will be greatly valued on the road to success.

Chapter XIII

PLANNING

PLANNING VS. PREPARATION

The ability to forge out of nothingness a desire result is not to be found. We must use the powers and forces at hand to our best advantage. This is the whole reason for planning: to get maximum results out of minimum effort. Economy is the prime directive in planning.

If the meek inherit the earth it will be because they have made plans. The meek understand that knowledge is the ultimate power. Foreknowledge is the advanced level of that power, enabling the activity of planning to find its fulfillment.

Preparation and planning are interrelated. Preparation is the singular mechanics of the plan and is inversely deductive in logic, where it is oriented to an end rather than a premise. When a plan is implemented we go to a particular element of the plan and prepare it, to cause the effect that fits the total image. Planning puts together various preparations so that an overall objective is achieved; therefore planning is inductive in its' logic. Preparation takes one item and changes things to that purpose. Planning organizes various preparations toward the entire scheme, fitting each one into its' place. Both planning and preparation help us to live with the disparity of our present circumstances, and the anxiety that raw waiting can generate. All plans are prepared and nearly all preparations are planned. The two activities cannot be viewed completely separate from each other. It is instructive to compare the different features of each, to help distinguish the emphasis the two procedures will have on some mental approaches. The following side-by-side list aids in this understanding:

PREPARATION	PLANNING
Purpose: to maximize effort and resources	**Purpose:** to maximize results; to minimize effort and resources.
Nature: more physical in application after prediction activity. (we prepare plans)	**Nature:** a mental activity done before physical activity. (we plan preparations)
Motivation: Fear, endurance, power, strength, skill etc.	**Motivation:** Want, desire, aspiration, vision etc.
Generating Future Event is unavoidable, generally external in origin.	**Generating Future Event** is in imagination and internal in origin.
Preparation secures fear and fosters confidence	**Planning** satisfies wants and establishes expectations.

Lack of preparation is more common that lack of planning. This fact will show the final difference. Preparation always requires an expenditure of energy and work. Planning does not require the physical expenditure of energy. Planning has mental operations as its emphasis, where preparation has physical operations as its emphasis; yet planning and preparation are really at their core a mental and mind process and procedure.

PREDICTION IMPROVES PLANNING

Specific knowledge of the future allows more creative planning and a reduction of forces and energy used to achieve the goals of any plan. When excessive variables and/or contingencies are present in a plan, it requires more provisions to ensure or secure a variable to allow positive action. This causes the need for greater amounts of energy to make action based on certain expectations. In this respect, prediction is seen as an economy in action. Good plans are based upon good prediction.

When predictions are derived from a particular mode, its distorting effect(s) will be reflected in the planning also. Further research may show that a person who favors a singular mode of approaching the future, will plan in this mode deductively. It might be said then, that there are **absolute** plans, **natural** plans, **imaginary** plans, **artificial** plans, **synthetic** plans, and **paradigm mode** plans. Our *plan* here is to use Futurlogics by not favoring any one approach. Planning done with the system of futurlogics is holistic planning, which simply put means that the future(s) used as a base for planning will be the broadest and most accurate possible. The goal and objective would be to plan from the **paradigm model**.

When our goals and objectives are motivating enough, we enter the assumptive mode with the ever-present elements of assumption, risk calculations characteristic of the artificial future and its originating mode are manifest. In these cases accurate prediction is not waited for. It means that the desired result of our plans so lure us to accept assumptions, rather than the more quiet statements of prediction meted out of **DMP**. Goals and objectives that are highly motivating poise us to consider the risks versus the gains—a common element in aggressive plans. At any rate, plans based upon assumptions and contingencies are more expensive to implement in the preparatory actions of the plan. Contingency planning is recursive and could easily consume all resources available to assure its success.

What ever type of preparation, planning, waiting, extended predicting we do or "engage in deeply," it is best to found it upon the broadest researched base of prediction possible, and thus avoiding modal restrictions that would distort all of the operations and activities, that we may have relative to the stimuli of the future. Futurlogics scan of the future is the preparatory step to planning. Predicting well is successful.

THE NATURAL BASE OF PLANNING

The things that will occur without the intervention of man are the natural base, and if each of us were the only person on Earth, then the natural base for any planning would be the natural future. In this hypothetical situation, anything that you might do would be the synthetic future. The synthetic future is founded upon the natural future caused by one person's presence and actions. In this simplistic situation, the *natural base* is the natural future and the synthetic future is our doing.

Yet, we are not alone on this planet, and the scope of the natural future and the natural base for plans should take into account the activities of our "shipmates," who share the planet with us. The natural base should take into its confines the synthetic future of all others as well, since what most men do is beyond control (if freedom is respected.) Therefore the synthetic future of all others could be accepted as natural events. Men are products of nature and are so enmeshed with natural events, that what man does must be seen as part of the natural future also. Nevertheless the natural base from which we begin our plans is not the same thing as the natural future. It is simply all that is beyond control of the planners, powers, and economies without plans.

This natural base is the backdrop against which we can contrast the things which will naturally occur, against the things that will require man's action, application of forces, control—to plan. Things which will not naturally occur become the subject of plans and preparations, and these may become our goals and our objectives, even the premise of our plan(s). The goals, objectives, aims are premise to planning.

GOALS AND THEIR ORIGIN

When the natural base has been determined preferably through Futurlogics, we select a goal or direction for the overall planning activity. We should always keep in mind the question, where do our goals, directives, requirements, objectives, aims, intent, etc., come from? The aims of preparation come from the natural base itself, as the thing that will occur naturally maybe a threat to the well-being and security of the individual, and he should do something to bolster himself to meet and endure the oncoming conditions/situation(s). But in planning, the negative opposite is the spur to the production of goals and objectives. For in determining the limits of the natural base we learn from it, that it will not provide us with the things we need, to achieve the level of success/goal that we desire. So if it is not provided naturally, we must create its occurrence. In the mind of man, if not the heart of man, will be the origin of all goals. If man were satisfied with the natural base he would not want to change anything, but would defend the continuance of the "status quo." Extreme environmentalism may be an example of this stance. Some however, want things to be better than they can be naturally, so they engineer the changes that fit their desires.

PURPOSE OF PLANS

The purpose of our plans therefore is, to cause something that would not occur naturally at the time we require it to become a reality. The tools of creativity find their employment here. And creativity requires imagination. Understanding the principle of imagination in creativity and discovery will reveal the origin of goals. Futurlogics requires the knowledge of the origin of every element of its operation

Goals find their genesis in our personality and in our motivational set. The contrast between our personality and our knowledge of the future will be the furnace, from which our goals and objectives will be drawn and determined, through "tempering experience."

It is true that our appetites and desires sometimes exceed our capacity to consume. Human beings are the only creatures on Earth who want more than is good for their purposes. This greed affects the kind and quality of goal selection. Intemperate choice of goals will have an effect or side effect on the outcome of plans. This greed comes from a lack of foresight and fear. We sometimes fear what we cannot see.

Goals should be reasonable and not strain the capacity of the planner, or the motivating effect of the goals will backlash and produce anxiety or be self defeating. If we set goals that are unreasonable, one of two things will occur:

A. It will stimulate the activity of preparation to bolster ourselves and seek power; our plans will become modal or preparatory.

B. It will cause strain through the pressure of the unrealistic goals, and this may engender a sense of failure. Failure is a poor base to further activities. Remember there is synergy in success. Nothing succeeds like success. Be successful to succeed.

Realistic goals should be kept within the scope of our resources and abilities. Many men have equal ability, but unequal resources, however unfortunate this may be, and it is a fact that must be considered with the process of goal selection. Ability can be seen as a resource, and nothing should be thought impossible, as pessimism kills the imagination which is the key to creative planning. The point is that, excessive failure is taken by some to be habit forming and frames much successive behavior. We can make good habits by good plans executed well.

INTELLIGENCE COMPENSATES FOR
LACK OF RESOURCES

An old saying reminds us that "the rich get richer" and this fact is hard to accept, let alone change. The rich get richer because of the available resources. In the traditional battle of "rich" versus "poor" we discover that the rich can achieve more because of the availability of resources, while the poor are so busy with a hand-to-mouth existence they have no time to set goals, even if they were to find a way of implementing them. Where resources are absent, intelligence must compensate for the lesser available resources. Intelligence is the greatest resource of all, and a man who is intelligent enough can do anything he desires. "Intelligent plans" are far superior to the "money plans" of the so called "rich." Intelligence is worth more than money.

Understanding laws and their effects makes it easier to overcome them. Often an imaginative and intelligent person seems to come from obscurity and makes his mark on history despite all opposition. We can learn much from these people. Compared to nature, even our most potent powers are feeble, and the laws that can produce success should be known by rich and poor alike. The less our resources, the greater should be our exercise of intelligence to achieve success. Good plans that are followed faithfully can offset the myth that only the rich get richer, because with a well thought out plan, the poor can become *rich* with execution of the plan. A good plan will get maximum results from minimum effort with diligence.

The intelligent person can, through proper planning, achieve success from proper preparations and goal selection. A rich person's plans can be outstripped by the vastly superior plans of the more intelligent person, who is rich in talent. The individual who uses available resources efficiently can also become rich. But until we have learned the proper application of planning, we should keep our goals reasonable and within reach, so that we can achieve the law that success is the best foundation for success. Deception is the greatest enemy of the synergy of a good plan. "Hot plans" are plans stressed by aggressive overreaching goals and objectives. "Cold plans" are plans with weak goals without proper challenge. "Warm plans" are plans that stimulate synergy and create energy. Do not be deceived by setting goals beyond practical usage—less is more.

RATIONALE BEHIND GOALS

Nevertheless, we should not limit ourselves. We should never undercut our potential. We should set goals and requirements that are commensurate with stimulating growth and progress. Although directed primarily toward the individual, these same principles apply to organizational goals as well. Under-achievement is a sense of failure also, so goals that focus plans to a result should bring harmony and potency to the overall plan. The art of setting goals should be tempered by the character of the participants of the plan. Plans should be understandable to all participants. Simple plans may be the best plan.

The leader of and organization should be aware that proper goal selection and assignments do not create unwanted stress and disrupting influences in the structure of the organization. An understanding of oneself is a good foundation to all levels and kinds of goal setting, both in the individual, the organization and in the leader.

The problems of social engineering and control of ideas and life styles are a tremendously complicated subject, where solutions though simple are hard to implement. But it is important in our investigation of goals and objectives and their origins, to question the social engineers. Where do their goals and objectives come from? What focuses their activities to promote their concepts of how "things" should be, for all of us who must ride the tide of their manipulations? The question of morality arises when we realize how their plans affect our lives and influence our goals, in order to comply with their efforts to produce their concept of society. We need to have our own goals and dreams.

What is our ultimate goal? A more abundant life! Positive plans with this as their ultimate goal, will always produce a measure of success, if they respect the personal volition of the individual.

LONG-RANGE PLANNING VS. SHORT-RANGE PLANNING

As we have discussed, the lack of resources and power can restrict or dampen the goals and objectives we select, constraining us to set our sights low in order to avoid the problem of trying to execute plans with inadequate means. We should not be broken, since there is a simple solution to maintain the Futurlogical approach and **DMP**. If we extend the plans by making those goals which require more resources than we presently have, the objects of *long-rang planning*, and delegate lesser goals to its subordinate *short-range planning,* forward thinking is maintained and **DMP** is not blocked by the restrictions of inadequacies or not enough resources, at the beginning.

We should have long-range plans, because they provide an overall framework from which we can base shorter term plans, we can more readily work with. This is most evident in large corporate organizations. The upper management plans for long-term goals which may extend from five to ten and more years into the future, and the middle management is assigned yearly or monthly goals, this, of course leaves the lowest ranking employee to deal with the day to day and/or week to week details, and the simple preparations of the plan under the supervision of the coordinating staff who ensure the proper feedback, to the overseers.

Long-range plans offer structure and pattern to the shorter planning activities. Implied in all planning is the sense that there are long-term priorities, because these make up the bank of assumptions and mathematical extrapolations (trends) of the status quo. Until Futurlogics, there has been no disciplined examination of the subconscious long-range plans we have. Long-range plans originate from the Paradigm Model of Futurlogics and Short-range plans originate from the Paradigm Mode. Long-range plans should be an extension of short-range plans.

Long-range plans will naturally affect short-range plans, but many short-rang plans we make daily can also give thrust to the long-range, as goals come from our motivational system. Being habitually shortsighted will influence goals we select, in longer term planning.

MAKING MODELS

Plans are models or symbolic representations of the synthetic future. It is from plans and their side effects that the synthetic future is generated. With plans we are able to simulate through prototype measures, the thing(s) that can be caused to happen. Thus, we find that in plans there will be models, blueprints, designs, drawings, whiteboard work, committees, brainstorm sessions, "barn raising(s)," tests, lab experiments, etc.. All of the techniques are to prototype the whole operation, so as to see ahead its successful potential. All these measures make a symbolic form of the plan in operation, to gain feedback before the more expensive and more strenuous work of the actual plan begins.

Miniaturization of the actual is a way of previewing the effectiveness of the plan. It is also a way of graphically representing the thoughts that plans are made of, since plans are abstract and difficult to deal with, and to interpret in concrete acts and schedules. Oftentimes, we fool ourselves into thinking we have thought of everything, but if we make a list in black and white of the things we intend to do, the mere effort of writing them down approaches the essentials of planning. To go ahead without clear and diagrammed exactness is also wasteful.

Few of us can do advanced mathematical problems in our head. We learn to write down the symbols and operations of the problem, so that we can free our mind to think of the solution realizing of course, that all the symbols and operation still only represent a number and their operatives. It is the same with planning, we cannot always think out the ways and means to accomplish our goals, so like the mathematician, we prototype them with models and miniature forms, so that we free our thought to make the most efficient approach to our goal actualization. Sometimes we have to hide the tree to see the forest.

Good plans are easy to understand or they are not the best plans. Good plans make thing understandable, which things might be misunderstood were it not for the planning efforts. The test is whether or not the plan communicates its essentials to all concerned. Without clear communication we work at cross purposes. We are deceive by ignorance traveling in several directions at once. Eventual goals may never be realized. Two persons seldom imagine an unreal thing in the same way. This does not imply, that to merely tell another person the plan, makes it viable. If we can communicate clearly even if it is only to ourselves, we lay out a means to an end. This is in harmony within rules, fact and laws. As with good prediction, good plans must be clear and understandable to all. All plans are abstractions until they are performed.

COMMITMENT STARTS THE ACTION

Good plans come from commitment. Commitment answers the question "What do you intend to do?" Commitment requires sacrifice. We believe if we expend time and energy on a project it seems a waste to break it off, so we become tied to our commitments through our sense of economy. If the value of our sacrifice is great enough, then the value of the plan becomes greater. Without sacrifice there is not commitment unless the participants do it out of joy and zeal.

If no plan is undertaken, no success can be expected. Whatever our motives, once underway there is an inertia that carries us on by its own. Of course if our commitment to the plan is feeble, the inertia to continue is feeble also.

After a recent presidential election, when years of planning resulted in success or in failure, both the winner and the loser may be asked, "What are your plans now?" The man who is on the ball will have a quick answer, but for the loser there is a "letdown" as everyone feels the total commitment to the cause of their party. Great men are always in the process of completing their plans, so if the mans is truly great, one loss is only a momentary setback, a mere rearrangement of his commitments. Greatness is not broken by loss.

Anyone who is at all interested in the future will have some degree of commitment to a plan, since all plans have something to do with the future. Even if your plan is to study the future in greater depth and organization. Most people have a difficult time finding value in the abstract, and once again the future is seen by many as largely abstract. Value is found in the hardware of everyday reality. Tomorrow is a dream that may never come. With this attitude commitment to the future is more problematic and not as enduring.

Time also is an abstraction. And the saying that "Time is money" makes it real. Even money is an abstraction sought after by us all. Many are committed to acquire as much of it as they can. The lack of materiality of the future should not be the deciding factor of value for the intelligent person. Learning to find value in non-material things, is a sign of maturity and farsightedness that lends itself to progress. The future is the reason for living.

We define time as a resource necessary for every plan. One of the first principles in planning is that we have enough time to plan and enough time to implement our plan. Planning with insufficient time shows improper prochronized events and prediction. While in the first steps of planning, we should predetermine the amount of time necessary to the success of that plan. This is fundamental with the course of complete planning. If we find that there is no time limit, this is a problem in itself, as no sense of motivation is felt. Here the time limits are assigned and set, to make commitment and motivation a contributing factor to the focus of the planning activity. When thing are under control, usually the amount of time required to accomplish our plans is within control also. In preparation, the time is externally set, while in planning it is more internally arranged.

BEING GUIDED BY THE PLAN

The operation and mental activity of planning itself is: to model and aid the mind toward the outcome of our plans. Extending the mind through the techniques of graphs, white boards, and layouts, computer modeling, help to keep clear the minute details that often are required to make a plan effective. Improvisation is not eliminated from planning but it is reduced to its practical use. The difference between a man acting out a plan and a man working off the top of his head, is marked by the difference between efficiency and critical indecision. A good plan has the form of preparation to meet the future with timing and focus of effective activity.

The two stages of planning are the creative stage and the execution stage. In the creative stage, the operations of the mind are enhanced to their limits. While in the execution stage the thought process is subdued, as it will interfere with direct and focused attention. The creative stage works with symbols, and the mechanical phase or execution stage works with action and things of the environment.

The synthetic future is therefore approached in two directions— the symbolic and mental, and the mechanical and material. If the synthetic future is kept only in the creative stages of planning, it will never become an actuality. This is tied into the principle of commitment. Commitment may be defined as setting direction to our motivations. Our motivations are never absent, but they sometimes work in directions other than conscious wishes. Once the plan is animated by the promise of the end result, the goal is seen as a reward for commitment— motivation is the result. Unless we are somehow motivated by planning, the synthetic future is never actualized.

Plans should be reduced to record, reference and guide activity. This reinforces the elemental consideration that a plan should be communicable. To prevent the plan from becoming cumbersome, it should be simple, quick, and accurate. Planning ahead avoids the problems of making decisions and choices, that should have been made beforehand. Planning ahead saves time and energy. Of course no plan can anticipate perfectly, and individual discretion and improvisation have a definite place. It is distasteful to think that being robots to a big plan destroys the most human thing we are—**thinkers**—but it is also unthinkable to waste resources and energy by not thinking ahead by getting a clear picture of what we should do, before we are overwhelmed by a deluge of unseen complications. When all things are equal the best thinkers wins. The best thinker think ahead and they have a plan to guide their further thinking. Thinking with a system such as Futurlogics should enhance thinking in general.

We learn to concentrate in order to overcome obstacles or solve problems. We think ahead so we do not need to think, when thinking would slow and cumber activity. Doing our thinking all at once and acting afterwards is a form of concentration. We concentrate the activity of thinking and we concentrate action to near reflex. Reflexive action is the best way of concentrating our powers. It is ridiculous to think we can do all things at once. We take turns to focus our actions where the force must be amplified to penetrate or move the obstacles.

Once plans have been followed and the desired results are obtained, then under the **same** conditions the plan will work again. This is what is called experience. The plan becomes knowledge and/or foreknowledge.

STEPS IN PLANNING

The synergy of planning cannot really be understood as a list of parts. To look at the principle of planning as anything less than a complete whole, is to leave out some of the most interesting dimensions of the activity. However, we can by separating the "operations" get a digestible portion of the whole. As we become more familiar, we can synthesize the parts to get the feel of the total activity.

❐ 1. To begin any planning, one should determine the mode with which the future is perceived. This may be from any single mode, but should be of the general overall modes/model of Futurlogics. Decisions and judgments variables can be simplified, if the mode of perception of the general and specific aspects of the future is known, during the mental stage of planning. Define natural base, that is "what will it be like if we do not plan or implement the plan?"

❏ 2. Goals, objective, missions, and requirements should be defined as well as results, effects, and desires, and these should be reduced to the terminology of change mechanics. No plan is effective until specific and single aims are set. Goals should focus the activity and complement the build-up of effects, that will cause the goal to be accomplished. We should see clearly where we want to go. The more clearly this is defined. The easier the plan will be developed.

❏ 3. Evaluation, appraisal, estimate of the present situation, is the logical pursuant to step two. After we can clearly see the goal as well as present circumstances. We can then inventory the elementary resources for implementing the plan(s).

❏ 4. Compare, analyze, and study the disparity between the present state and the future stage/state desired or required. The future state of *goals achieved*, is compared to the present state of *goals yet to be achieved*. The changes needed to achieve the plan's *end result*, should be more evident.

❏ 5. Will the ad quo occur naturally or will intervention and energy be required to overcome obstacles and bring about the desired change at the right time? Resources at hand should be evaluated to determine, if they will be sufficient. If they are deficient, external sources must be explored. Our commitment is now determined so that we can direct activity appropriately.

❏ 6. Set the time requirements and structuring. Schedules and the sense of time, use and passage, is an essential activity. Planning organizes all the activities relative to the future and puts them into a system. What the concert is to the single musician the activity of planning is to any single activity such as waiting. Waiting activity is the scheduling the time to accomplish the goal.

❏ 7. Communicate to all who will participate the requirements to accomplish subgoals/goals. Organize, coordinate all subgoals and overall plans that systematize them into a complete, encompassing plan. Some planning begins with many specific plans that are combined in an overall super-plan. In this case, the sub-plans are formed first and the main plan organizes them. The other case is that a main plan may be so complex that in order to communicate the minor requirements to the participants, subgoals are generated to guide the subordinate activities of the constituent faction of the implementing staff.

❑ 8. Set up a monitoring feedback system to have obstacle and unforeseen events brought to the fore so that a resolution may be effected within time standards. One may set watchful eyes upon any contingency areas so that he will not be caught off guard.

❑ 9. Plan the equilibrium or life expectancy of the desired results. Once you have accomplished the goal, how long do you desire that condition to remain? If you desire only to get to the top of the mountain, then as soon as you get there you can turn around and return, saying that the goal is accomplished. But if you wish to clear a jungle for farming, you may want a permanent condition that makes permanent farming possible, and the constant fight of the encroaching jungle might prove to be an expensive output that prohibits any further agricultural projects.

DEALING WITH THE FUTURE THROUGH PLANNING

The main thread that runs through all the efforts of planning is economy. We must use tactical considerations from minimum output to get maximum results. The fear often inherent in prospective thinking is lessened through planning. The present level of civilization has not come by accident. Much thought and study has gone into making the best use of the available powers. The concept of the "trigger"—the smaller force controlling the larger force—is the key to our present power over our environment. Knowledge of the future enhances our awareness of "triggers" and when to use them for maximum economy.

Brute force is necessary, but intelligent use of force is the key to getting the above mentioned "triggering action." Plans set up the planning is eliminating the obstacles which prevent the satisfaction of our needs and desires. Our own strength is often insufficient to overcome or eliminate this opposition to our acquisition of selected goals.

The opposite to "triggering" is sampling and attenuation. Here, we have the larger forces to move and guide smaller forces. This is mainly a concept of perception and sensing. All the indication and instrumentation are based upon attenuation and sampling. At the base of perception is intelligence. The laws of intelligence are fundamental ingredients of planning and of activities relative to the future.

If we were unable to cause things to happen we would not be able to plan. We would only be able to predict. In our discussion of the synthetic future, we used the hand to illustrate the mind's extension to material surroundings. We could then say that a person with no hands would not plan, because he could not cause anything to happen. The mind of man would be helpless without the "helping" hand to carry out his plan. Prediction is saying what *will happen* through observation. Planning enables us say what we may *cause to happen.*

As we gain more power to cause things to happen, we will predict less and plan more. The acquisition of power over our environment is steadily increasing. Therefore, we should see an increase in people working under the guide of different levels of planning. To understand the nature of the plan makes understanding the motives and reasons for our behavior easier.

The temptations of multinational corporations to ensure the success of their plans by exercising force and market manipulation is significant in light of our discussion of the relationship of power and the intellectual process of prediction.   Mind over material things is one thing, but mind over mankind is another. It is historically evident that we have dominated or used the weak to obtain power. Self-expression is an admirable quest, but if we infringe upon the self-expression of others this turns freedom into slavery.   Man shaping man and social engineering, propaganda, political manipulation of the few ruling the many are serious problems that will emerge from the increase of power available to us. Plans with power should be understood so freedom can be preserved.

Looking ahead, many have anticipated the increase of our power over the environment. Because of this, many contingency plans are now devised based upon these "ifs."   When the power is realized and available for use, then these potential plans become viable. This is a case where prediction makes possible the development of plans in advance of their need, so that the time needed for planning can be assured. The more "ifs" we have to base the future upon, the greater our need to assure the contingency levels of our plans are minimal. Contingency planning is motivated by the enticement of reward. Power to reduce the "contingency variable" to the "actionable certain" is the thrust of the quest for power to insure the success of any plan.

OBSTACLES AND THE PLANNING ATTITUDE

❏ 1. People who are not committed by a plan are seen to be free. Planning is synonymous to commitment. We find that there is an identification to planning as a lack of freedom. This is an illusion. If we are not committed to the workings of some plan, we are subject to forces that would overwhelm us. Planning uses the powers we have more effectively. Planning if properly used, is a force in itself. Planning requires thought, and thought is a force. Any means that aids that force is freedom. There are plans to keep us free and there are plans to bring us under a tyrant. The attitude behind the plan is the difference. The purpose of planning is to have greater freedom and efficiency to obtain our goals and commitment if use properly will not destroy the entrepreneurial spirit. We still have to be flexible to modify the plan.

❏ 2. As with all human behavior, planning is rooted in habit. Overcoming the habits of avoidance is one of the first things we should do, to improve our innate skills of planning and creativity. Get the habit of being prompt, creative, flexible, future-minded and positive.

❏ 3. When a commitment is made, it always means that there is an inherent sacrifice or limitation. This implies a contest of self-control versus self-indulgence. Some, if not all tend to be *now oriented* to some degree and this is how we lose awareness of the future and/or the past, which are the other dimensions of the temporal environment.

❏ 4. Planning is thinking, and true thinking is work. Work is a demand seen as a sacrifice rather than an opportunity to exercise our faculties of being. We should be aware that there are always limits and balances in all things. There some things not to be sacrificed such virtue, common sense, love, meditation, work etc..

❏ 5. The Artificial Future is an obstacle, especially when it is wrong and rooted in strong emotions. Plans based upon the negative side of the artificial future will eventually mean self-discovery, and this is a difficult thing for most people to face. A beneficial artificial future however is a vision to motivate us and builds self-esteem.

❏ 6. Planning takes time, and this time of thoughtful preparation is viewed by some as laziness. There is no need to feel guilty taking time to plan, as it will save time in the long run, and the long run will get us, the farthest, the fastest. "A stitch in time save nine," "Think before you act," really is a help.

❐ 7. When one is confronted with a task that is beyond the capacity of simple hard work, one should look for a way to accomplish the goal which will be more effective than just "digging in." The person should know where to dig, how long, with what and when. Work for work is exercise, but work for profit is success. Success should pilot the ship of all our plans. Planning is not laziness, but potential work.

DECISION, TIME, AND RESOURCES

Decisions come from our awareness of the range and limitation of powers. Knowing what we can and cannot do clearly is the key to making speedy decisions. If the exact nature of our resources and powers is always hazy, decisions will be difficult and filled with anxiety. A simple aid to decision making will be to first define our capabilities, potential, resources, etc. in the initial planning activity. This kind of inventory should be realistic, or the effect will compound the problems rather than ease them.

These same limitations force upon us the requirement to make accurate predictions with enough time, to make preparations and plans to increase our powers. Foreknowledge enables us to use the leverage principle in approaching any future event. The sooner we know of some future event, the more time we have to organize and focus the existing forces, in order to amplify their effects, if needed.

All decision(s) making has a degree of foretelling inherent to the process. Looking at the consequences of possible alternatives can aid, in the selection of one course of action over another. Sometimes it requires setting down priorities, so that selection does not mean exclusion of one or the other, rather it is a matter of taking turns and ordering a schedule as the time approaches. At any rate, without some knowledge of what will be, decisions would be just an act of caprice. We should act with purpose and direction toward goals. Remember again Futurlogics does not care if we can actually predict or see the future in actuality, as we have a *future* because it is part of our mental makeup. Whether the future is real or a figment of imagination—it matters not!

We should look at the decision-making process as an opportunity to see what we believe the future to be, or what we know it can be. It should be during this time that we make our most extensive reaches into the future, and feel, and perceive what it might be. We should be introspective, and discover what **DMP** is really about.

Decisions are always associated with anxiety or cognitive dissonance. Paradoxically, decisions made are always seen as cathartic and a relief. Nevertheless planning will always involve decisions, and decision will be fraught with angst. We have to decide to make decisions.

The word decision means to "cut" or "cut out" from the whole. Generally speaking one of two alternatives is to be "cut out," and the remaining to be worked with as the resolution. If we could do all things at once, then the process of deciding would not be necessary. But we cannot do all things at once. In order to do anything at all, we select a course of action and work to accomplish it. When we would like to do both, but are conscious of our limits and resources, we must sometimes sacrifice one goal to acquire the other or extend our plan to include both.

Commitment means sacrifice. To stick with our commitments is to maintain a direction at the expense of other possibilities or directions. Therefore, to sacrifice an alternative is to commit ourselves to something else. The ancient law of sacrifice was really, in effect, a test of commitment to the Jewish law and covenant. In today's terms, sacrifice concerns time and money. The college student whose tuition is paid is not as dedicated as the student who must pay his own way, given they both love learning equally. The strength of our commitment is described in our willingness to sacrifice, or our desire to remain resolute.

There are four kinds of decisions. One is a choice between two positives. Another is a choice between two negatives. Third is to choose a negative in preference to a positive, and fourth is to choose a positive over a negative. All of these decisions while not ideally desired are required of us, because of the real nature of the world and our sense of limitations. Or perhaps real limitations.

Often a decision is made only to avoid making another decision. Some persons would rather meet the frustrations of wrong choices, than to work the process of decision making, and face the humiliation of reality. We should avoid the tendency to escape into our decisions, as it leads to more complex decisions later. Make the good decision early, it will help prevent this type of complication. The earlier we can come to our decisions, the greater the leverage factor of foreknowledge.

PLANS MAKE MEN EQUAL

To summarize, a man with a plan can head off problems in advance, and this is an advantage over the man who improvises in a surprise. We literally should plan every activity of our lives. If we do this with a good spirit we can experience great degrees of progress. Plans make leaders. The largest share of improvisation we do, should be in our moments of planning, and not in the desperation at the moment of occurrence. If you work well under pressure then more power be with you. Planning if done to accommodate your style could even help those who work best in a surprise. The pressure should be to plan fast.

UNIVERSAL ENGINEERING

Planning is the most general form of engineering. All other forms of engineering become mere technical activities. In this age of the specialist, where one studies so much about small aspects of the total environment, and nothing is tied into the larger scope, Futurlogics becomes a handbook of the universal engineer. Planning is the most creative of all future-minded activities, and is therefore involved in the motivations and psyche of the human mind in the most imaginative way. All specialists today must find their direction with the overall generalist of the future. The problems of unguided specialists inputting into the environment with no notion of the future effects, has been aptly described in Alvin Toffler's book, FUTURE SHOCK. We need universal planners. Futurlogics is the best engineering handbook for the futurist, who seeks to set aright the chaotic disregard for side effects, and those who use side effects to social(ly) engineer society.

IT IS THE BEGINNING!

PRAXIS

Some say that prediction of the future is just a guess. Taking this postulate to the extreme, let us look at the operation of the human guess. Can one guess like an explosion in sheer randomness? Of course random with no shaping or influences, is only an imaginary event. Yet even imagination has "fluences" (Weibull Distribution.) And there is bouncing off each other, an object or energy interact(s), even if it is against each other in the mix of things. There are collisions.

There is "in the mix of things" these classification of guesses and more:

educated guess	prosaic guess	common sense guess
biased guess	preconditioned guess	denying guess
ignorant guess	knowledgeable guess	naïve guess
expert guess	studied evaluated guess	lucky guess
esp guess	spiritual guess	inspired guess
pre-influenced guess	random guess	hysterical guess
crazed guess	"cooked" guess	chaotic guess
lustful guess	hopeful guess	blasphemous guess
divine guess	disparate guess	calculated guess
blind guess	"dumb" guess	gambled guess
memory guess	system guess	intuitive guess
insightful guess	stupid guess	human guess
guessing games	swag (acronym)	lucky guess
guessing based upon previous guess(es)		

Guesses in school are controlled. Students are not rewarded for guessing in tests. They are ridiculed when they offer ideas not always drawn from assigned study. Guessing is seen to be an evidence of poor preparation or poor teaching. Never or seldom are they seen as ideas coming from intuitive thoughts, from free association, from insightful or intuitive feelings, structures, or approaches. Discipline and order prevail. Chaos disturbs the teaching environment.

We as living beings can not guess by shear randomness . There is always Weibull distribution in the human condition . Guessing is useful to the futurist, as they are clues to the method(s) used to futur.

The purpose for Futurlogics is to increase the "hit success" of our guessing. So that guessing gains a greater respect, or becomes authoritative and impressive to the skeptic with greater accuracy. Guessing makes futuring useful.

Funny Farm © 1988 movie excerpt:

Moving guy: Hey Mac, which way to Redbud?
Mac: How'd you know my name was Mac?
Moving guy: Just guessed.
Mac: Then why don't you guess your way to Redbud.

Futurist guesses are influenced by following sample list :

- Family
- Cultural
- Economics
- Personality
- Thoughts
- Health

- Linguistics
- Sociology
- Education(s)
- Paradigms
- Dreams
- Religion

After the futurist has enough guesses. The *next* step would be to categorize them into such sample categories as:

- Crazy
- Ridiculous
- Never happen, impossible.
- Never happen, possible
- May happen, possible
- Possible
- Probable
- Highly Probable
- Likely
- Pending
- Certain
- Inevitable
- Future Reality
- Eternal Reality

Then the futurist offers various imaginative scenarios based upon the above categories. Possibilities considered.

Then the futurist ponders over the most suitable scenario(s) and that is—he makes judgments. Probabilities weighed.

Then the futurist "dry labs" preparations, plans dependent upon the above scenario(s) to proof the scenarios, doing risk assessments vs reward assessments. This is the place for mind experiments and ROI Return On Investment analysis. Where will all this go?

Next tactical to strategic preparation/planning begins if it is a bottom up style. Or Strategic to tactical planning/preparations begins if it is top down style. Or Strategic to tactical and then tactical to strategic if is is middle out style. Use this paradigm to view future(s).

If it is impossible to predict the future, then all efforts of futuring are a philosophical exercise, as opposed to the direct prediction by some ESP, PRECOGNITION, FUTURE CONSCIOUSNESS. Such things are avoided and never directly address, but "shrunk from" and "apologized for" and "dismissed or disrespected" or are "out of the rules" of futuring. They are beyond the game of future studies. No religion! No spiritual awakenings! Strict Observational Mode and Natural Future! The Synthetic Future is driven by technological utopia. This open denial of the spiritual, is central to the world society of futurists.

Since many methodologies are based upon the various philosophies concerning the "knowability" of the future or future(s). What are the various denials or avoidance mechanisms in prediction of the future? Or in Futurlogics view, what are their **modes**?

No matter what the various beliefs futurist have concerning the methods of discovering the future(s). There are "lone wolf futurist" with his own methods, to and including the "peer reviewed societal futurist" with widely accepted methods. Though they have different strategies, internal mental structures, methods to futur the future, they will eventually come to a system like Futurlogics—after all the guessing is done. This prediction is an extrapolation from current trends in futurism.

EPILOGUE

LEADERSHIP AND FORETHOUGHT

If all our lives we remain but followers of the vision of others, the need to look ahead would just be an academic study. Our social structure as a free society demands more than this blindness. It demands our initiative to make the organization more flexible and adaptable to change. If nothing ever changed once leaders gave directives, these rules and laws would suffice conceivably forever, becoming tradition. Needless to say, change is a constant element of existence.

It is because of the ever present factor of change, that leadership—and forethought—are needed. No organization is perfect, therefore as new and unusual situations are encountered by the subordinate, he will immediately call his supervisor for correct policy and procedure. Business and social organizations are constantly looking for competent leadership, to handle the constant flux of change. Traditions require tuning after all.

In the lower echelons of an organization, the rules, guides, and goals are given by the "boss." Everything is a matter of following information handed down by the higher levels of management. The future of the lowest level of a social hierarchy will be dealing with brief excursions into the future, as in the case of the assembly-line worker, who must concentrate on the item he is assembling and only cast his attention ahead as far as the next item to be built, in a serial of repetition.

As persons rise to higher and higher positions in the business world and in the social structure, dealing with the future becomes more direct and intense. Positions such as the board of directors, planning committees, presidents of companies, think tanks etc., are usually in close contact with problems that require a long range view, to handle the immediate prospects. Towards the top of any social structure, the future becomes a permanent challenge.

This then, becomes a rule of thumb in management structures: the higher up the management ladder one climbs, the greater the amount of time must be spent in thoughts concerning the future, and the greater is the responsibility to prepare/plan to meet inevitable change.

AT THE VERY TOP

Where do those in uppermost positions of leadership get the rules and directives, they issue to those below them? What kind of future do they envision as the result of their decisions? The followers are disciplined to obey those in command, but the leader is self-disciplined to what? The soldier obeys his officers, but where does the general get his orders in the chain of command? These are important questions to consider, since no one can or should lead without some notion or view of the future. What/who informs their views?

We would not need leaders, but only rules and traditions, if it were not for change. A smoothly running organization may work unhampered in ordinary circumstances, but when people are surprised by change, they run at wits end and shrug responsibility and cover their tracks. Leaders are created when someone ends up shouldering the responsibility, and stands out to be seen and heard. Society has found that things run better, when important and long-reaching decisions are made by the upper levels of virtue, talent and mentality. It is in the rarefied atmosphere of the mind and heart that we find answers, to where the leader gets his information. This book is intended to be used by future leaders and those at the upper levels of social structures, for consideration of long range future matters, that concern us all.

The future-minded person cannot help but be elevated to an eventual position of leadership, if his technique get things done. By studying the future, one must learn the principles found in leadership, government, and social engineering. No one who studies the future can remain a follower for very long. Everyone should study the future to be free and progress to our full potential and to fulfill our dreams.

SOCIAL ENGINEERING

When those who are in authority attempt to engineer the present social structure to some different life style, we find that we are subject to their ideas of what is best for us. They though they will deny it, have a future which they use as a map or model, to which they would force us to conform. Sometimes they do these things so subtly, that by the time we realize what they are doing, we cannot change the effects of their plans. The announced goals of their plans are not their intention, as the "side effects" of their plan are the real goal. Social engineering differs from government and leadership, in that the people under social engineering are not aware of the ultimate consequences of their proposals. They use the side effects of their programs and agencies to promote their ultimate goals, ostensibly for our good.

Doing things for the good of people is moral action. Morals however, are not claimed as a motive in their science. This then, is a contradiction. The purpose of religion is to inculcate moral principles, which should if all people were to embrace them, bring about a social order of peace, prosperity, happiness. The current social engineers claim that they exist without religious connotations. If they have no religious motives, then they must imagine an ultimate future for society that is fashioned to their own designs.

We need to know what the future which they would design for us "looks like," to remain free. By discovering how people learn and operate under the stimulus of their mental view of the future, we have also discovered that the modes of the future are many. Social engineers like the rest of us, have their favorite modes. Futurlogics would make sure that what others are doing for "our good," do not bring unexpected consequences. We need to know our personal futures to choose.

Futurlogics is a point from which we can gauge the ideals and motives of those who would influence our lives. We have learned that ones' conception of the future is directly related to the motivational systems of the human personality. If we are to recognize good leaders and beneficial social reforms, we should look at the future and at the motives of the people who intend to bring about the changes, which we should have decided for ourselves.

GOVERNMENT IDEALS

When we select officials for our government we must look to the future, to see possible consequences of their policies and practices. We should ask them, "what do they see for the country in the next few years?" If their view seems hazy or unclear we might doubt their capability to fill the offices, the people will depend upon in the later years of their administration. We should not want a fabulous artificial future, but a viable vision all will sustain.

If a government is truly by the people, then for that government to accomplish its goals, it must have an educated populace from which to draw its leaders. Voters who know nothing about the future(s) will not make the best choice to fill leadership positions. The populace of a nation should know the future(s) envisioned for their nation. They must recognize the people who will help them to accomplish that vision. Remember the future is our ultimate goal! And it should be our choice.

THE BIRTH OF FUTURLOGICS

Futurlogics is an infant, but with nourishment it will grow and mature. We may see it as a perfect approach to the future as others add to this humble imperfect start. Omissions and errors can be excused, if we realize that there have been no precedents, except in ancient times. Futurlogics invites everyone's creative thought and perspective towards improving Futurlogics *the system of prospective thinking*.

What is **FUTURLOGICS?** It is a **MOS**. A **MOS** or *(M)ind (O)perating (S)ystem* is the theme upon which we execute our methods or praxis. It is how we apply our knowledge either upon knowledge itself, or upon the things we know are about to be. It is theory in action.

THE *SCIENCE* OF PREDICTION,
THE *ART* OF FORETELLING,
THE *GIFT* OF PROPHECY

The **Science of Prediction** is developed from an observational method of treatment. It is all the conscious operation of the mind used to obtain information and data, that will enable us to tell beforehand, what should happen if conditions remain the same.

The **Art of Foretelling** is the art of drawing from the subconscious means in addition to the conscious mental processes. Since emotions and feelings—and perhaps dreams—are involved, it is more complicated, and it reaches the state of an art. The rules and procedures of prognostication are learned, the same as any artful endeavor.

The **Gift of Prophecy** relies upon the highest levels of intelligence. It exists in a rarefied atmosphere, and it is understood only at that altitude.

All three ways of prognostication should be in harmony. They ought not to contend with each other. One is not superior to another. They support one another by reinforcing the prescience of the other. Each has its limitations, but this means that when one reaches its limits another should come to its aid.

The outside proof of any statement of the future (besides waiting to see) is found in the corroboration of the other means. The gift helps the science and the science helps the gift. Proving anything we learn of the future is by prediction in other forms. Seldom is prediction made certain by immediate circumstances. A prediction is proved by better prediction. Foretelling is proved by the gift of prophecy. What proves the gift of prophecy? The gifted. If the ability to prophesy is possible in everyone, then the principles of Futurlogics will be perfected.

Descarte postulated "cogito, ergo sum:" "I think, therefore I am." If thinking proves ones existence, what turns mere existence into life? Beyond existence, quality of life, personal growth, success must be predicated upon *prospective thinking*. ...

ABOUT THE AUTHOR AS Of 1983

James Norman Hall was born in Salt Lake City, Utah. He works for an international computer company and lives on a half-acre home site in Utah. His wife, Julie, is from Mexico City, and the couple has two cultures to share with their family of six children.

This book is the result of many years of note-taking as James brainstormed futurism (which is just now beginning to boom in interest across the country,) and the idea of codifying his findings in the form of a book about prospective thought began about eight years ago. FUTURLOGICS contains useful and unique principles of psychology, and has bearings on decision making and dealing with the problems of the future. James does not see himself as a mystic or a clairvoyant, rather he views himself to be a thinker, involved in private research of an up-and-coming discipline. Direct Mental Process or Direct Mind Perception, **DMP** is the simple child-like open mindedness we must achieve, to eliminate the prejudicing effect of things we have held to be true, but which must shortly be revised.

BOOKS by james n hall and Julie O. Hall as of 2013:

PYRAMIDS OF GOD

Thinking Paradigms of Light and Truth © 2007 © 2010

> **Subject matter:** *Pyramids of God is an application of* **Futurlogics**
>
> Written by james n. hall with Julie O. Hall

SEARCH ISAIAH חפש ישעיהו

Pyramid ZERO The Witness and Poetry of Isaiah © 2010

> **Subject matter:** *Search Isaiah is an application of the Pyramids of God which is an application of* **Futurlogics** *used to bring to understanding the writings of the premier futurist, prophet, poet ISAIAH*
>
> *Written by james n. hall with Julie O. Hall*

More information on **Futurlogics** at http://www.futurlogics.com

POSTSCRIPT

There is great intrinsic beauty in the rainbow that is seen in the clear aftermath of a storm-cleansing rain. If the sun is shining its even white light is splayed out in the luminescent colors. Everyone can see the reward of heaven, for putting up with the moment of dark clouds and thundering flashings of the clouds, in pondering thoughts. Just as the mind rains upon us knowledge once in a while, the mind will also display before the bright light of consciousness, a thing of great beauty. These special moments which more than pay for the brooding of a thoughtful mind, are like the clouds that once dispelled make room for the rainbow, we wait for in search of knowledge and understanding.

Futurlogics then becomes a prism that takes the light of consciousness within each of us, and portrays a spectrum of thought that rivals the tints in the rainbow. If each mode and future is seen as the complementary colors of white light, then **DMP**'s total impact may be anticipated.

The climate and weather of the planet Earth, in some respects, have been easier to predict than the events of man. The societies' times and seasons could also be predictable, if we understood mankind. Man measures man against himself; someday as the arrow of progress continues its flight upward, the greatest value in the universe will be found. That thing of greatest worth will be the charitable heart. A society where kindness prevails will be the most knowledgeable ever. Perhaps the storms of today's changes and conditions, will give way to a rainbow of promise. All who penetrate the future see good things. Only they who do not respect others, see the gloom.

When the roots of the ARTIFICIAL FUTURE are discerned, the size of the tree can be measured. The future then is like a tree with many branches and leaves to catch the sun, and roots to absorb the rains.

1983

It has been thirty years since Futurlogics was first published. It has had great impact in our lives and our thinking. It is part of our soul.
james n. hall and Julie O. Hall   **2013**

HISTORY *as a point of reference for charting the course ahead is obsolete. Soon absolutes will become mere variables. New tools are needed to prepare for the times ahead.*

FUTURLOGICS *is an expanding spiral of thought to organize and systemize all the principles of thinking future through* *DMP.*

PREDICTING, PREPARING, PLANNING *with the understanding gained through reading this handbook will liberate the mind to think as it should.*